**OTHER BOOKS B**

Available on Amazon

**Claim These Free Resources that Will Help You Unleash the Power of Your Words and Speak with Confidence. Visit www.speakforsuccesshub.com/toolkit for Access.**

### 18 Free PDF Resources

### 30 Free Video Lessons

### 2 Free Workbooks

**Claim These Free Resources that Will Help You Unleash the Power of Your Words and Speak with Confidence. Visit www.speakforsuccesshub.com/toolkit for Access.**

## 18 Free PDF Resources

*12 Iron Rules for Captivating Story, 21 Speeches that Changed the World, 341-Point Influence Checklist, 143 Persuasive Cognitive Biases, 17 Ways to Think On Your Feet, 18 Lies About Speaking Well, 137 Deadly Logical Fallacies, 12 Iron Rules For Captivating Slides, 371 Words that Persuade, 63 Truths of Speaking Well, 27 Laws of Empathy, 21 Secrets of Legendary Speeches, 19 Scripts that Persuade, 12 Iron Rules For Captivating Speech, 33 Laws of Charisma, 11 Influence Formulas, 219-Point Speech-Writing Checklist, 21 Eloquence Formulas*

## 30 Free Video Lessons

We'll send you one free video lesson every day for 30 days, written and recorded by Peter D. Andrei. Days 1-10 cover authenticity, the prerequisite to confidence and persuasive power. Days 11-20 cover building self-belief and defeating communication anxiety. Days 21-30 cover how to speak with impact and influence, ensuring your words change minds instead of falling flat. Authenticity, self-belief, and impact – this course helps you master three components of confidence, turning even the most high-stakes presentations from obstacles into opportunities.

## 2 Free Workbooks

We'll send you two free workbooks, including long-lost excerpts by Dale Carnegie, the mega-bestselling author of *How to Win Friends and Influence People* (5,000,000 copies sold). *Fearless Speaking* guides you in the proven principles of mastering your inner game as a speaker. *Persuasive Speaking* guides you in the time-tested tactics of mastering your outer game by maximizing the power of your words. All of these resources complement the Speak for Success collection.

# THE

# PSYCHOLOGY

# OF

# COMMUNICATION

### THE UNDERGROUND GUIDE TO PERSUASIVE
### PRESENTATIONS AND EASY ELOQUENCE

*Peter Andrei*

# THE

# PSYCHOLOGY

# OF

# COMMUNICATION

### SPEAK FOR SUCCESS COLLECTION BOOK

# XIV

SPEAK
TRUTH
WELL
# PRESS

A SUBSIDIARY OF SPEAK TRUTH WELL LLC
800 Boylston Street
Boston, MA 02199

**SPEAK**
**TRUTH**
**WELL LLC**

SPEAK FOR SUCCESS COLLECTION

Printed in the United States of America
40 39 38 37 36 35 34 33 32 31

While the author has made every effort to provide accurate internet addresses at the time of publication, neither the publisher nor the author assumes any responsibility for errors, or for changes that occur after publication. Further, the publisher does not have any control over and does not assume any responsibility for author or third-party websites or their content.

www.speakforsuccesshub.com/toolkit

## FREE RESOURCES FOR OUR READERS

We believe in using the power of the internet to go above and beyond for our readers. That's why we created the free communication toolkit: 18 free PDF resources, 30 free video lessons, and even 2 free workbooks, including long-lost excerpts by Dale Carnegie, the mega-bestselling author of *How to Win Friends and Influence People*. (The workbooks help you put the most powerful strategies into action).

**We know you're busy. That's why we designed these resources to be accessible, easy, and quick. Each PDF resource takes just 5 minutes to read or use. Each video lesson is only 5 minutes long. And in the workbooks, we bolded the key ideas throughout, so skimming them takes only 10 minutes each.**

Why give so much away? For three reasons: we're grateful for you, it's useful content, and we want to go above and beyond. Questions? Feel free to email Peter directly at pandreibusiness@gmail.com.

www.speakforsuccesshub.com/toolkit

# WHY DOES THIS HELP YOU?

### I

The PDF resources cover topics like storytelling, logic, cognitive biases, empathy, charisma, and more. You can dig deeper into the specific topics that interest you most.

### II

Many of the PDF resources are checklists, scripts, example-compilations, and formula-books. With these practical, step-by-step tools, you can quickly create messages that work.

### III

With these free resources, you can supplement your reading of this book. You can find more specific guidance on the areas of communication you need to improve the most.

### IV

The two workbooks offer practical and actionable guidance for speaking with complete confidence (*Fearless Speaking*) and irresistible persuasive power (*Persuasive Speaking*).

### V

You can even learn from your phone with the free PDFs and the free video lessons, to develop your skills faster. The 30-lesson course reveals the secrets of building confidence.

### VI

You are reading this because you want to improve your communication. These resources take you to the next level, helping you learn how to speak with power, impact, and confidence. We hope these resources make a difference. They are available here:

www.speakforsuccesshub.com/toolkit

From the desk of Peter Andrei
Speak Truth Well LLC
800 Boylston Street
Boston, MA 02199
pandreibusiness@gmail.com

May 15, 2021

**What is Our Mission?**

To whom it may concern:

The Wall Street Journal reports that public speaking is the world's biggest fear – bigger than being hit by a car. According to Columbia University, this pervasive, powerful, common phobia can reduce someone's salary by 10% or more. It can reduce someone's chances of graduating college by 10% and cut their chances of attaining a managerial or leadership position at work by 15%.

If weak presentation kills your good ideas, it kills your career. If weak communication turns every negotiation, meeting, pitch, speech, presentation, discussion, and interview into an obstacle (instead of an opportunity), it slows your progress. And if weak communication slows your progress, it tears a gaping hole in your confidence – which halts your progress.

Words can change the world. They can improve your station in life, lifting you forward and upward to higher and higher successes. But they have to be strong words spoken well: rarities in a world where most people fail to connect, engage, and persuade; fail to answer the question "why should we care about this?"; fail to impact, inspire, and influence; and, in doing so, fail to be all they could be.

Now zoom out. Multiply this dynamic by one thousand; one million; one billion. The individual struggle morphs into a problem for our communities, our countries, our world. Imagine the many millions of paradigm-shattering, life-changing, life-saving ideas that never saw the light of day. Imagine how many brilliant convictions were sunk in the shipyard. Imagine all that could have been that failed to be.

Speak Truth Well LLC solves this problem by teaching ambitious professionals how to turn communication from an obstacle into an engine: a tool for converting "what could be" into "what is." There is no upper limit: inexperienced speakers can become self-assured and impactful; veteran speakers can master the skill by learning advanced strategies; masters can learn how to outperform their former selves.

We achieve our mission by producing the best publications, articles, books, video courses, and coaching programs available on public speaking and communication, and at non-prohibitive prices. This combination of quality and accessibility has allowed Speak Truth Well to serve over 70,000 customers in its year of launch alone (2021). Grateful as we are, we hope to one day serve millions.

Dedicated to your success,

Peter Andrei
President of Speak Truth Well LLC
pandreibusiness@gmail.com

# PROLOGUE:

*This three-part prologue reveals my story, my work, and the practical and ethical principles of communication. It is not a mere introduction. It will help you get more out of the book. It is a preface to the entire 15-book Speak for Success collection. It will show you how to use the information with ease, confidence, and fluency, and how to get better results faster. If you would like to skip this, flip to page 50, or read only the parts of interest.*

## I

*page XIII*

**MY STORY AND THE STORY OF THIS COLLECTION**

*how I discovered the hidden key to successful communication, public speaking, influence, and persuasion*

## II

*page XXIV*

**THE 15-BOOK SPEAK FOR SUCCESS COLLECTION**

*confidence, leadership, charisma, influence, public speaking, eloquence, human nature, credibility - it's all here*

## III

*page XXIX*

**THE PRACTICAL TACTICS AND ETHICAL PRINCIPLES**

*how to easily put complex strategies into action and how to use the power of words to improve the world*

# I

## MY STORY AND THE STORY OF THIS COLLECTION

*how I discovered the hidden key to successful communication, public speaking, influence, and persuasion (by reflecting on a painful failure)*

## HOW TO GAIN AN UNFAIR ADVANTAGE IN YOUR CAREER, BUSINESS, AND LIFE BY MASTERING THE POWER OF YOUR WORDS

I WAS SITTING IN MY OFFICE, TAPPING A PEN against my small wooden desk. My breaths were jagged, shallow, and rapid. My hands were shaking. I glanced at the clock: 11:31 PM. "I'm not ready." Have you ever had that thought?

I had to speak in front of 200 people the next morning. I had to convince them to put faith in my idea. But I was terrified, attacked by nameless, unreasoning, and unjustified terror which killed my ability to think straight, believe in myself, and get the job done.

Do you know the feeling?

After a sleepless night, the day came. I rose, wobbling on my tired legs. My head felt like it was filled with cotton candy. I couldn't direct my train of thoughts. A rushing waterfall of unhinged, self-destructive, and meaningless musings filled my head with an uncompromising cacophony of anxious, ricocheting nonsense.

"Call in sick."

"You're going to embarrass yourself."

"You're not ready."

I put on my favorite blue suit – my "lucky suit" – and my oversized blue-gold wristwatch; my "lucky" wristwatch.

"You're definitely not ready."

"That tie is ugly."

"You can't do this."

The rest went how you would expect. I drank coffee. Got in my car. Drove. Arrived. Waited. Waited. Waited. Spoke. Did poorly. Rushed back to my seat. Waited. Waited. Waited. Got in my car. Drove. Arrived home. Sat back in my wooden seat where I accurately predicted "I'm not ready" the night before.

Relieved it was over but disappointed with my performance, I placed a sheet of paper on the desk. I wrote "MY PROBLEMS" at the top, and under that, my prompt for the evening: "What did I do so badly? Why did everything feel so off? Why did the speech fail?"

"You stood in front of 200 people and looked at... a piece of paper, not unlike this one. What the hell were you thinking? You're not fooling anyone by reading a sentence and then looking up at them as you say it out loud. They know you're reading a manuscript, and they know what that means. You are unsure of yourself. You are unsure of your message. You are unprepared. Next: Why did you speak in that odd, low, monotone voice? That sounded like nails on a chalkboard. And it was inauthentic. Next: Why did you open by talking about yourself? Also, you're not particularly funny. No more jokes. And what was the structure of the speech? It had no structure. That, I feel, is probably a pretty big problem."

I believed in my idea, and I wanted to get it across. Of course, I wanted the tangible markers of a successful speech. I wanted action. I wanted the speech to change something in the real world. But my motivations were deeper than that. I wanted to see people "click" and come on board my way of thinking. I wanted to captivate the audience. I wanted to speak with an engaging, impactful voice, drawing the audience in, not repelling them. I wanted them to remember my message and to remember me. I wanted to feel, for just a moment, the thrill of power. But not the petty, forceful power of tyrants and dictators; the justified power – the earned power – of having a good idea and conveying it well; the power of Martin Luther King and John F. Kennedy; a power harnessed in service of a valuable idea, not the personal privilege of the speaker. And I wanted confidence: the quiet strength that comes from knowing your words don't stand in your way, but propel you and the ideas you care about to glorious new mountaintops.

Instead, I stood before the audience, essentially powerless. I spoke for 20 painful minutes – painful for them and for me – and then sat down. I barely made a dent in anyone's consciousness. I generated no excitement. Self-doubt draped its cold embrace over me. Anxiety built a wall between "what I am" and "what I could be."

I had tried so many different solutions. I read countless books on effective communication, asked countless effective communicators for their advice, and consumed countless courses on powerful public speaking. Nothing worked. All the "solutions" that didn't really solve my problem had one thing in common: they treated communication as an abstract art form. They were filled with vague, abstract pieces of advice like "think positive thoughts" and "be yourself." They confused me more than anything else. Instead of illuminating the secrets I had been looking for, they shrouded the elusive but indispensable skill of powerful speaking in uncertainty.

I knew I had to master communication. I knew that the world's most successful people are all great communicators. I knew that effective communication is the bridge between "what I have" and "what I want," or at least an essential part of that bridge. I knew that without effective communication – without the ability to influence, inspire, captivate, and move – I would be all but powerless.

I knew that the person who can speak up but doesn't is no better off than the person who can't speak at all. I heard a wise man say "If you can think and speak and write, you are absolutely deadly. Nothing can get in your way." I heard another wise man say "Speech is power: speech is to persuade, to convert, to compel. It is to bring another out of his bad sense into your good sense." I heard a renowned psychologist say "If you look at people who are remarkably successful across life, there's various reasons. But one of them is that they're unbelievably good at articulating what they're aiming at and strategizing and negotiating and enticing people with a vision forward. Get your words together... that makes you unstoppable. If you are an effective writer and speaker and communicator, you have all the authority and competence that there is."

When I worked in the Massachusetts State House for the Department of Public Safety and Homeland Security, I had the opportunity to speak with countless senators, state representatives, CEOs, and other successful people. In our conversations, however brief, I always asked the same question: "What are the ingredients of your success? What got you where you are?" 100% of them said effective communication. There was not one who said anything else. No matter their field – whether they were entrepreneurs, FBI agents, political leaders, business leaders, or multimillionaire donors – they all pointed to one skill: the ability to convey powerful words in powerful ways. Zero exceptions.

Can you believe it? It still astonishes me.

My problem, and I bet this may be your obstacle as well, was that most of the advice I consumed on this critical skill barely scratched the surface. Sure, it didn't make matters worse, and it certainly offered some improvement, but only in inches when I needed progress in miles. If I stuck with the mainstream public speaking advice, I knew I wouldn't unleash the power of my words. And if I didn't do that, I knew I would always accomplish much less than I could. I knew I would suffocate my own potential. I knew I would feel a rush of crippling anxiety every time I was asked to give a presentation. I knew I would live a life of less fulfillment, less success, less achievement, more frustration, more difficulty, and more anxiety. I knew my words would never become all they could be, which means that I would never become all I could be.

To make matters worse, the mainstream advice – which is not wrong, but simply not deep enough – is everywhere. Almost every article, book, or course published on this subject falls into the mainstream category. And to make matters worse, it's almost impossible to know that until you've spent your hard-earned money and scarce time with the resource. And even then, you might just shrug, and assume that shallow, abstract advice is all there is to the "art" of public speaking. As far as I'm concerned, this is a travesty.

I kept writing. "It felt like there was no real motive; no real impulse to action. Why did they need to act? You didn't tell them. What would happen if they didn't? You didn't tell them that either. Also, you tried too hard to put on a formal façade; you spoke in strange, twisted ways. It didn't sound sophisticated. And your mental game was totally off. You let your mind fill with destructive, doubtful, self-defeating thoughts. And your preparation was totally backward. It did more to set bad habits in stone than it did to set you up for success. And you tried to build suspense at one point but revealed the final point way too early, ruining the effect."

I went on and on until I had a stack of papers filled with problems. "That's no good," I thought. I needed solutions. Everything else I tried failed. But I had one more idea: "I remember reading a great speech. What was it? Oh yeah, that's right: JFK's inaugural address. Let me go pull it up and see why it was so powerful." And that's when everything changed.

I grabbed another sheet of paper. I opened JFK's inaugural address on my laptop. I started reading. Observing. Analyzing.

Reverse-engineering. I started writing down what I saw. Why did it work? Why was it powerful? I was like an archaeologist, digging through his speech for the secrets of powerful communication. I got more and more excited as I kept going. It was late at night, but the shocking and invaluable discoveries I was making gave me a burst of energy. It felt like JFK – one of the most powerful and effective speakers of all time – was coaching me in his rhetorical secrets, showing me how to influence an audience, draw them into my narrative, and find words that get results.

"Oh, so that's how you grab attention."

"Aha! So, if I tell them this, they will see why it matters."

"Fascinating – I can apply this same structure to my speech."

Around 3:00 in the morning, an epiphany hit me like a ton of bricks. That night, a new paradigm was born. A new opportunity emerged for all those who want to unleash the unstoppable power of their words. This new opportunity changed everything for me and eventually, tens of thousands of others. It is now my mission to bring it to millions, so that good people know what they need to know to use their words to achieve their dreams and improve the world.

Want to hear the epiphany?

**The mainstream approach**: Communication is an art form. It is unlike those dry, boring, "academic" subjects. There are no formulas. There are no patterns. It's all about thinking positive thoughts, faking confidence, and making eye contact. Some people are naturally gifted speakers. For others, the highest skill level they can attain is "not horrible."

**The consequences of the mainstream approach**: Advice that barely scratches the surface of the power of words. Advice that touches only the tip of the tip of the iceberg. A limited body of knowledge that blinds itself to thousands of hidden, little-known communication strategies that carry immense power; that blinds itself to 95% of what great communication really is. Self-limiting dogmas about who can do what, and how great communicators become great. Half the progress in twice the time, and everything that entails: missed opportunities, unnecessary and preventable frustration and anxiety, and confusion about what to say and how to say it. How do I know? Because I've been there. It's not pretty.

**My epiphany, the new Speak for Success paradigm**: Communication is as much a science as it is an art. You can study words that changed the world, uncover the hidden secrets of their power, and apply these proven principles to your own message. You can discover precisely what made great communicators great and adopt the same strategies. You can do this without being untrue to yourself or flatly imitating others. In fact, you can do this while being truer to yourself and more original than you ever have been before. Communication is not unpredictable, wishy-washy, or abstract. You can apply predictable processes and principles to reach your goals and get results. You can pick and choose from thousands of little-known speaking strategies, combining your favorite to create a unique communication approach that suits you perfectly. You can effortlessly use the same tactics of the world's most transformational leaders and speakers, and do so automatically, by default, without even thinking about it, as a matter of effortless habit. That's power.

**The benefits of the Speak for Success paradigm**: Less confusion. More confidence. Less frustration. More clarity. Less anxiety. More courage. You understand the whole iceberg of effective communication. As a result, your words captivate others. You draw them into a persuasive narrative, effortlessly linking your desires and their motives. You know exactly what to say. You know exactly how to say it. You know exactly how to keep your head clear; you are a master of the mental game. Your words can move mountains. Your words are the most powerful tools in your arsenal, and you use them to seize opportunities, move your mission forward, and make the world a better place. Simply put, you speak for success.

Fast forward a few years.

I was sitting in my office at my small wooden desk. My breaths were deep, slow, and steady. My entire being – mind, body, soul – was poised and focused. I set my speech manuscript to the side. I glanced at the clock: 12:01 AM. "Let's go. I'm ready."

I had to speak in front of 200 people the next morning. I had to convince them to put faith in my idea. And I was thrilled, filled with genuine gratitude at the opportunity to do what I love: get up in front of a crowd, think clearly, speak well, and get the job done.

I slept deeply. I dreamt vividly. I saw myself giving the speech. I saw myself victorious, in every sense of the word. I heard applause. I saw their facial expressions. I rose. My head was clear. My mental game was pristine. My mind was an ally, not an obstacle.

"This is going to be fun."

"I'll do my best, and whatever happens, happens."

"I'm so lucky that I get to do this again."

I put on my lucky outfit: the blue suit and the blue-gold watch.

"Remember the principles. They work."

"You developed a great plan last night. It's a winner."

"I can't wait."

The rest went how you would expect. I ate breakfast. Got in my car. Drove. Arrived. Waited. Waited. Waited. Spoke. Succeeded. Walked back to my seat. Waited. Waited. Waited. Got in my car. Drove. Arrived home. Sat back in my wooden seat where I accurately predicted "I'm ready" the night before.

I got my idea across perfectly. My message succeeded: it motivated action and created real-world change. I saw people "click" when I hit the rhetorical peak of my speech. I saw them leaning forward, totally hushed, completely absorbed. I applied the proven principles of engaging and impactful vocal modulation. I knew they would remember me and my message; I engineered my words to be memorable. I felt the thrilling power of giving a great speech. I felt the quiet confidence of knowing that my words carried weight; that they could win hearts, change minds, and help me reach the heights of my potential. I tore off the cold embrace of self-doubt. I defeated communication anxiety and broke down the wall between "what I am" and "what I could be."

Disappointed it was over but pleased with my performance, I placed a sheet of paper on the desk. I wrote "Speak Truth Well" and started planning what would become my business.

To date, we have helped tens of thousands of people gain an unfair advantage in their career, business, and life by unleashing the power of their words. And they experienced the exact same transformation I experienced when they applied the system.

If you tried to master communication before but haven't gotten the results you wanted, it's because of the mainstream approach; an approach that tells you "smiling at the audience" and "making eye contact" is all you need to know to speak well. That's not exactly a malicious lie – they don't know any better – but it is completely incorrect and severely harmful.

If you've been concerned that you won't be able to become a vastly more effective and confident communicator, I want to put those fears to rest. I felt the same way. The people I work with felt the same way. We just needed the right system. One public speaking book written by the director of a popular public speaking forum – I won't name names – wants you to believe that there are "nine public speaking secrets of the world's top minds." Wrong: There are many more than nine. If you feel that anyone who would boil down communication to just nine secrets is either missing something or holding it back, you're right. And the alternative is a much more comprehensive and powerful system. It's a system that gave me and everyone I worked with the transformation we were looking for.

Want to Talk? Email Me:

**PANDREIBUSINESS@GMAIL.COM**

This is My Personal Email.
I Read Every Message and
Respond in Under 12 Hours.

Visit Our Digital Headquarters:

**WWW.SPEAKFORSUCCESSHUB.COM**

See All Our Free Resources, Books, Courses, and Services.

# II

## THE 15-BOOK SPEAK FOR SUCCESS COLLECTION

*confidence, leadership, charisma, influence, public speaking, eloquence, human nature, credibility – it's all here, in a unified collection*

## MASTER EVERY ASPECT OF COMMUNICATION

T HE BESTSELLING SPEAK FOR SUCCESS COLLECTION covers every aspect of communication. Each book in the collection includes diagrams that visualize the essential principles, chapter summaries that remind you of the main ideas, and checklists of the action items in each section, all designed to help you consult the set as a reference.

This series is a cohesive, comprehensive set. After writing the first book, I realized how much information I couldn't fit into it. I wrote the second. After writing the second, the same thing happened. I wrote the third. The pattern continued. As of this writing, there are fifteen books in the collection. After writing each book, I felt called to write another. It is the ultimate communication encyclopedia.

Aside from a small amount of necessary overlap on the basics, each book is a distinct unit that focuses on an entirely new set of principles, strategies, and communication secrets. For example, *Eloquence* reveals the secrets of language that sounds good; *Trust is Power* reveals the secrets of speaking with credibility; *Public Speaking Mastery* reveals a blueprint for delivering speeches.

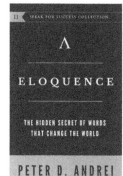

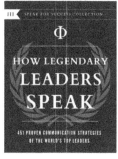

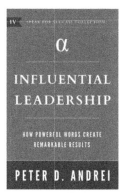

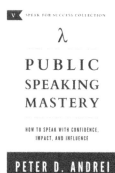

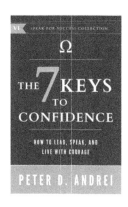

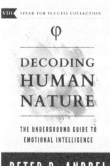

"The most complete and comprehensive collection of communication wisdom ever compiled." – *Amazon Customer*

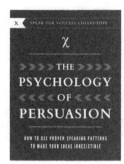
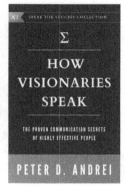
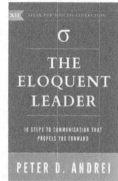

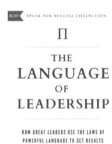

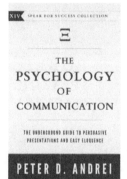

*"I love the diagrams and summary checklists. I have all 15 on my shelf, and regularly refer back to them."* – *Amazon Customer*

## You Can Learn More Here:
## www.speakforsuccesshub.com/series

......................................A Brief Overview.................................

- I wrote *How Highly Effective People Speak* to reveal the hidden patterns in the words of the world's most successful and powerful communicators, so that you can adopt the same tactics and speak with the same impact and influence.

- I wrote *Eloquence* to uncover the formulas of beautiful, moving, captivating, and powerful words, so that you can use these exact same step-by-step structures to quickly make your language electrifying, charismatic, and eloquent.

- I wrote *How Legendary Leaders Speak* to illuminate the little-known five-step communication process the top leaders of the past 500 years all used to spread their message, so that you can use it to empower your ideas and get results.

- I wrote *Influential Leadership* to expose the differences between force and power and to show how great leaders use the secrets of irresistible influence to develop gentle power, so that you can move forward and lead with ease.

- I wrote *Public Speaking Mastery* to shatter the myths and expose the harmful advice about public speaking, and to offer a proven, step-by-step framework for speaking well, so that you can always speak with certainty and confidence.

- I wrote *The 7 Keys to Confidence* to bring to light the ancient 4,000-year-old secrets I used to master the mental game and speak in front of hundreds without a second of self-doubt or anxiety, so that you can feel the same freedom.

- I wrote *Trust is Power* to divulge how popular leaders and career communicators earn our trust, speak with credibility, and use this to rise to new heights of power, so that you can do the same thing to advance your purpose and mission.

- I wrote *Decoding Human Nature* to answer the critical question "what do people want?" and reveal how to use this knowledge to develop unparalleled influence, so that people adopt your idea, agree with your position, and support you.

- I wrote *Influence* to unearth another little-known five-step process for winning hearts and changing minds, so that you can know with certainty that your message will persuade people, draw support, and motivate enthusiastic action.

- I wrote *The Psychology of Persuasion* to completely and fully unveil everything about the psychology behind "Yes, I love it! What's the next step?" so that you can use easy step-by-step speaking formulas that get people to say exactly that.

- I wrote *How Visionaries Speak* to debunk common lies about effective communication that hold you back and weaken your words, so that you can boldly share your ideas without accidentally sabotaging your own message.

- I wrote *The Eloquent Leader* to disclose the ten steps to communicating with power and persuasion, so that you don't miss any of the steps and fail to connect, captivate, influence, and inspire in a crucial high-stakes moment.

- I wrote *The Language of Leadership* to unpack the unique, hidden-in-plain-sight secrets of how presidents and world-leaders build movements with the laws of powerful language, so that you use them to propel yourself forward.

- I wrote *The Psychology of Communication* to break the news that most presentations succeed or fail in the first thirty seconds and to reveal proven, step-by-step formulas that grab, hold, and direct attention, so that yours succeeds.

- I wrote *The Charisma Code* to shatter the myths and lies about charisma and reveal its nature as a concrete skill you can master with proven strategies, so that people remember you, your message, and how you electrified the room.

- **Learn more: www.speakforsuccesshub.com/series**

# III

## PRACTICAL TACTICS AND ETHICAL PRINCIPLES

*how to easily put complex strategies into action and how to use the power of words to improve the world in an ethical and effective way*

## MOST COMMUNICATION BOOKS

HAVE YOU READ ANOTHER BOOK ON COMMUNICATION? If you have, let me remind you what you probably learned. And if you haven't, let me briefly spoil 95% of them. "Prepare. Smile. Dress to impress. Keep it simple. Overcome your fears. Speak from the heart. Be authentic. Show them why you care. Speak in terms of their interests. To defeat anxiety, know your stuff. Emotion persuades, not logic. Speak with confidence. Truth sells. And respect is returned."

There you have it. That is most of what you learn in most communication books. None of it is wrong. None of it is misleading. Those ideas are true and valuable. But they are not enough. They are only the absolute basics. And my job is to offer you much more.

Einstein said that "if you can't explain it in a sentence, you don't know it well enough." He also told us to "make it as simple as possible, but no simpler." You, as a communicator, must satisfy both of these maxims, one warning against the dangers of excess complexity, and one warning against the dangers of excess simplicity.

And I, as someone who communicates about communication in my books, courses, and coaching, must do the same.

## THE SPEAK FOR SUCCESS SYSTEM

The Speak for Success system makes communication as simple as possible. Other communication paradigms make it even simpler. Naturally, this means our system is more complex. This is an unavoidable consequence of treating communication as a deep and concrete science instead of a shallow and abstract art. If you don't dive into learning communication at all, you miss out. I'm sure you agree with that. But if you don't dive *deep*, you still miss out.

### THE FOUR QUADRANTS OF COMMUNICATION

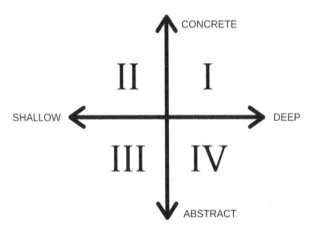

FIGURE VIII: There are four predominant views of communication (whether it takes the form of public speaking, negotiation, writing, or debating is irrelevant). The first view is that communication is concrete and deep. The second view is that communication is concrete and shallow. The third view is that communication is shallow and abstract. The fourth view is that communication is deep and abstract.

## WHAT IS COMMUNICATION?

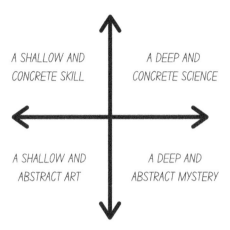

FIGURE VII: The first view treats communication as a science: "There are concrete formulas, rules, principles, and strategies, and they go very deep." The second view treats it as a skill: "Yes, there are concrete formulas, rules, and strategies, but they don't go very deep." The third view treats it as an art: "Rules? Formulas? It's not that complicated. Just smile and think positive thoughts." The fourth view treats it as a mystery: "How are some people such effective communicators? I will never know..."

## WHERE WE STAND ON THE QUESTION

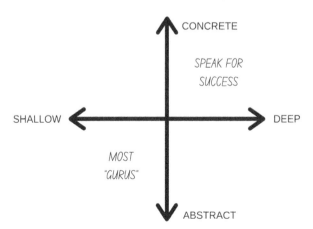

FIGURE VI: Speak for Success takes the view that communication is a deep and concrete science. (And by "takes the view," I mean "has discovered.") Most other communication writers, thought-leaders, public speaking coaches, and individuals and organizations in this niche treat communication as a shallow and abstract art.

This doesn't mean the Speak for Success system neglects the basics. It only means it goes far beyond the basics, and that it doesn't turn simple ideas into 200 pages of filler. It also doesn't mean that the Speak for Success system is unnecessarily complex. It is as simple as it can possibly be.

In this book, and in the other books of the Speak for Success collection, you'll find simple pieces of advice, easy formulas, and straightforward rules. You'll find theories, strategies, tactics, mental models, and principles. None of this should pose a challenge. But you'll also find advanced and complicated strategies. These might.

What is the purpose of the guide on the top of the next page? To reveal the methods that make advanced strategies easy. When you use the tactics revealed in this guide, the difficulty of using the advanced strategies drops dramatically. They empower you to use complicated and unfamiliar persuasive strategies with ease. If the 15-book Speak for Success collection is a complete encyclopedia of communication, to be used like a handbook, then this guide is a handbook for the handbook.

### A SAMPLING OF EASY AND HARD STRATEGIES

| Easy and Simple | Hard and Complicated |
|---|---|
| Use Four-Corner Eye Contact | The Fluency-Magnitude Matrix |
| Appeal to Their Values | The VPB Triad |
| Describe the Problem You Solve | The Illusory Truth Effect |
| Use Open Body Language | Percussive Rhythm |
| Tell a Quick Story | Alliterative Flow |
| Appeal to Emotion | Stacking and Layering Structures |
| Project Your Voice | The Declaratory Cascade |
| Keep it as Simple as Possible | Alternating Semantic Sentiments |

# THE PRACTICAL TACTICS

---◆◇◆---

R ECOGNIZE THAT, WITH PRACTICE, YOU can use any strategy extemporaneously. Some people can instantly use even the most complex strategies in the Speak for Success collection after reading them just once. They are usually experienced communicators, often with competitive experience. This is not an expectation, but a possibility, and with practice, a probability.

CREATE A COMMUNICATION PLAN. Professional communication often follows a strategic plan. Put these techniques into your plan. Following an effective plan is not harder than following an ineffective one. Marshall your arguments. Marshall your rhetoric. Stack the deck. Know what you know, and how to say it.

DESIGN AN MVP. If you are speaking on short notice, you can create a "minimum viable plan." This can be a few sentences on a notecard jotted down five minutes before speaking. The same principle of formal communication plans applies: While advanced strategies may overburden you if you attempt them in an impromptu setting, putting them into a plan makes them easy.

MASTER YOUR RHETORICAL STACK. Master one difficult strategy. Master another one. Combine them. Master a third. Build out a "rhetorical stack" of ten strategies you can use fluently, in impromptu or extemporaneous communication. Pick strategies that come fluently to you and that complement each other.

PRACTICE THEM TO FLUENCY. I coach a client who approached me and said he wants to master every strategy I ever compiled. That's a lot. As of this writing, we're 90 one-hour sessions in. To warm up for one of our sessions, I gave him a challenge: "Give an impromptu speech on the state of the American economy, and after you stumble, hesitate, or falter four times, I'll cut you off. The challenge is to see how long you can go." He spoke for 20 minutes without a single mistake. After 20 minutes, he brought the impromptu speech to a perfect, persuasive, forceful, and eloquent conclusion. And he naturally and fluently used advanced strategies throughout his impromptu speech. After he closed the speech (which he did because he wanted to get on with the session), I asked him if he thought deeply about the strategies he used. He said no. He used them thoughtlessly. Why? Because he practiced them. You can too. You can practice them on your own. You don't need an audience. You don't need a coach. You don't even need to speak. Practice in your head. Practice ones that resonate with you. Practice with topics you care about.

KNOW TEN TIMES MORE THAN YOU INTEND TO SAY. And know what you do intend to say about ten times more fluently than you need to. This gives your mind room to relax, and frees up cognitive bandwidth to devote to strategy and rhetoric in real-time. Need to speak for five minutes? Be able to speak for 50. Need to read it three times to be able to deliver it smoothly? Read it 30 times. INCORPORATE THEM IN SLIDES. You can use your slides or visual aids to help you ace complicated strategies. If you can't remember the five steps of a strategy, your slides can still follow them. Good slides aren't harder to use than bad slides. USE THEM IN WRITTEN COMMUNICATION. You can read your speech. In some situations, this is more appropriate than impromptu or extemporaneous speaking. And if a strategy is difficult to remember in impromptu speaking, you can write it into your speech. And let's not forget about websites, emails, letters, etc. PICK AND CHOOSE EASY ONES. Use strategies that come naturally and don't overload your mind. Those that do are counterproductive in fast-paced situations. TAKE SMALL STEPS TO MASTERY. Practice one strategy. Practice it again. Keep going until you master it. Little by little, add to your base of strategies. But never take steps that overwhelm you. Pick a tactic. Practice it. Master it. Repeat. MEMORIZE AN ENTIRE MESSAGE. Sometimes this is the right move. Is it a high-stakes message? Do you have the time? Do you have the energy? Given the situation, would a memorized delivery beat an impromptu, in-the-moment, spontaneous delivery? If you opt for memorizing, using advanced strategies is easy. USE ONE AT A TIME. Pick an advanced strategy. Deliver it. Now what? Pick another advanced strategy. Deliver it. Now another. Have you been speaking for a while? Want to bring it to a close? Pick a closing strategy. For some people, using advanced strategies extemporaneously is easy, but only if they focus on one at a time. MEMORIZE A KEY PHRASE. Deliver your impromptu message as planned, but add a few short, memorized key phrases throughout that include advanced strategies. CREATE TALKING POINTS. Speak from a list of pre-written bullet-points; big-picture ideas you seek to convey. This is halfway between fully impromptu speaking and using a script. It's not harder to speak from a strategic and persuasively-advanced list of talking points than it is to speak from a persuasively weak list. You can either memorize your talking points, or have them in front of you as a guide. TREAT IT LIKE A SCIENCE. At some point, you struggled with a skill that you now perform effortlessly. You mastered it. It's a habit. You do it easily, fluently, and thoughtlessly. You can do it while you daydream. Communication is the same. These tactics, methods, and strategies are not supposed to be stuck in the back of your mind as you speak. They are supposed to be ingrained in your habits. RELY ON FLOW. In fast-paced and high-stakes situations, you usually don't plan every word, sentence, and idea consciously and deliberately. Rather, you let your subconscious mind take over. You speak from a flow state. In flow, you may flawlessly execute strategies that would have overwhelmed your conscious mind. LISTEN TO THE PROMPTS. You read a strategy and found it difficult to use extemporaneously. But as you speak, your subconscious mind gives you a prompt:

"this strategy would work great here." Your subconscious mind saw the opportunity and surfaced the prompt. You execute it, and you do so fluently and effortlessly. FOLLOW THE FIVE-STEP CYCLE. First, find truth. Research. Prepare. Learn. Second, define your message. Figure out what you believe about what you learned. Third, polish your message with rhetorical strategies, without distorting the precision with which it conveys the truth. Fourth, practice the polished ideas. Fifth, deliver them. The endeavor of finding truth comes before the rhetorical endeavor. First, find the right message. Then, find the best way to convey it.

CREATE YOUR OWN STRATEGY. As you learn new theories, mental models, and principles of psychology and communication, you may think of a new strategy built around the theories, models, and principles. Practice it, test it, and codify it.

STACK GOOD HABITS. An effective communicator is the product of his habits. If you want to be an effective communicator, stack good communication habits (and break bad ones). This is a gradual process. It doesn't happen overnight.

DON'T TRY TO USE THEM. Don't force it. If a strategy seems too difficult, don't try to use it. You might find yourself using it anyway when the time is right.

KNOW ONLY ONE. If you master one compelling communication strategy, like one of the many powerful three-part structures that map out a persuasive speech, that can often be enough to drastically and dramatically improve your impact.

REMEMBER THE SHORTCOMING OF MODELS. All models are wrong, but some are useful. Many of these complex strategies and theories are models. They represent reality, but they are not reality. They help you navigate the territory, but they are not the territory. They are a map, to be used if it helps you navigate, and to be discarded the moment it prevents you from navigating.

DON'T LET THEM INHIBIT YOU. Language flows from thought. You've got to have something to say. And *then* you make it as compelling as possible. And *then* you shape it into something poised and precise; persuasive and powerful; compelling and convincing. Meaning and message come first. Rhetoric comes second. Don't take all this discussion of "advanced communication strategies," "complex communication tactics," and "the deep and concrete science of communication" to suggest that the basics don't matter. They do. Tell the truth as precisely and boldly as you can. Know your subject-matter like the back of your hand. Clear your mind and focus on precisely articulating exactly what you believe to be true. Be authentic. The advanced strategies are not supposed to stand between you and your audience. They are not supposed to stand between you and your authentic and spontaneous self – they are supposed to be integrated with it. They are not an end in themselves, but a means to the end of persuading the maximum number of people to adopt truth. Trust your instinct. Trust your intuition. It won't fail you.

## MASTERING ONE COMMUNICATION SKILL

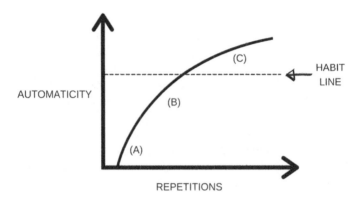

FIGURE V: Automaticity is the extent to which you do something automatically, without thinking about it. At the start of building a communication habit, it has low automaticity. You need to think about it consciously (A). After more repetitions, it gets easier and more automatic (B). Eventually, the behavior becomes more automatic than deliberate. At this point, it becomes a habit (C).

## MASTERING COMMUNICATION

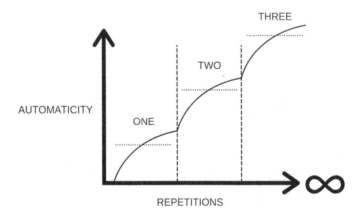

FIGURE IV: Layer good communication habits on top of each other. Go through the learning curve over and over again. When you master the first good habit, jump to the second. This pattern will take you to mastery.

## THE FOUR LEVELS OF KNOWING

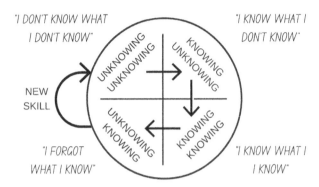

FIGURE III: First, you don't know you don't know it. Then, you discover it and know you don't know it. Then, you practice it and know you know it. Then, it becomes a habit. You forget you know it. It's ingrained in your habits.

## REVISITING THE LEARNING CURVE

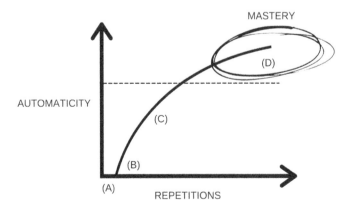

FIGURE II: Note the stages of knowing on the learning curve: unknowing unknowing (A), knowing unknowing (B), knowing knowing (C), unknowing knowing (D).

## WHAT'S REALLY HAPPENING?

Have you ever thought deeply about what happens when you communicate? Let's run through the mile-high view.

At some point in your life, you bumped into an experience. You observed. You learned. The experience changed you. Your neural networks connected in new ways. New rivers of neurons began to flow through them.

The experience etched a pattern into your neurobiology representing information about the moral landscape of the universe; a map of *where we are, where we should go, and how we should make the journey.* This is meaning. This is your message.

Now, you take the floor before a crowd. Whether you realize it or not, you want to copy the neural pattern from your mind to their minds. You want to show them where we are, where we should go, and how we should make the journey.

So, you speak. You gesture. You intone. Your words convey meaning. Your body language conveys meaning. Your voice conveys meaning. You flood them with a thousand different inputs, some as subtle as the contraction of a single facial muscle, some as obvious as your opening line. Your character, your intentions, and your goals seep into your speech. Everyone can see them. Everyone can see you.

Let's step into the mind of one of your audience members. Based on all of this, based on a thousand different inputs, based on complex interactions between their conscious and nonconscious minds, the ghost in the machine steps in, and by a dint of free will, acts as the final arbiter and makes a choice. A mind is changed. You changed it. And changing it changed you. You became more confident, more articulate, and deeper; more capable, more impactful, and stronger.

Communication is connection. One mind, with a consciousness at its base, seeks to use ink or pixels or airwaves to connect to another. Through this connection, it seeks to copy neural patterns about the present, the future, and the moral landscape. Whatever your message is, the underlying connection is identical. How could it not be?

## IS IT ETHICAL?

By "it," I mean deliberately using language to get someone to do or think something. Let's call this rhetoric. We could just as well call it persuasion, influence, communication, or even leadership itself.

The answer is yes. The answer is no. Rhetoric is a helping hand. It is an iron fist. It is Martin Luther King's dream. It is Stalin's nightmare. It is the "shining city on the hill." It is the iron curtain. It is "the pursuit of happiness." It is the trail of tears. It is "liberty, equality, and brotherhood." It is the reign of terror. Rhetoric is a tool. It is neither good nor evil. It is a reflection of our nature.

Rhetoric can motivate love, peace, charity, strength, patience, progress, prosperity, common sense, common purpose, courage, hope, generosity, and unity. It can also sow the seeds of division, fan the flames of tribalism, and beat back the better angels of our nature.

Rhetoric is the best of us and the worst of us. It is as good as you are. It is as evil as you are. It is as peace-loving as you are. It is as hate-mongering as you are. And I know what you are. I know my readers are generous, hardworking people who want to build a better future for themselves, for their families, and for all humankind. I know that if you have these tools in your hands, you will use them to achieve a moral mission. That's why putting them in your hands is my mission.

Joseph Chatfield said "[rhetoric] is the power to talk people out of their sober and natural opinions." I agree. But it is also the power to talk people out of their wrong and harmful opinions. And if you're using rhetoric to talk people out of their sober opinions, the problem isn't rhetoric, it's you.

In the *Institutes of Rhetoric*, Roman rhetorician Quintilian wrote the following: "The orator then, whom I am concerned to form, shall be the orator as defined by Marcus Cato, a good man, skilled in speaking. But above all he must possess the quality which Cato places first and which is in the very nature of things the greatest and most important, that is, he must be a good man. This is essential not merely on account of the fact that, if the powers of eloquence serve only to lend arms to crime, there can be nothing more pernicious than eloquence to public and private welfare alike, while I myself, who have labored to the best of my ability to contribute something of the value to oratory, shall have rendered the worst of services to mankind, if I forge these weapons not for a soldier, but for a robber."

Saint Augustine, who was trained in the classical schools of rhetoric in the 3rd century, summed it up well: "Rhetoric, after all, being the art of persuading people to accept something, whether it is true or false, would anyone dare to maintain that truth should stand there without any weapons in the hands of its defenders against falsehood; that those speakers, that is to say, who are trying to convince their hearers of what is untrue, should know how to get them on their side, to gain their attention and have them eating out of their hands by their opening remarks, while these who are defending the truth should not? That those should utter their lies briefly, clearly, plausibly, and these should state their truths in a manner too boring to listen to, too obscure to understand, and finally too repellent to believe? That those should attack the truth with specious arguments, and assert falsehoods, while these should be incapable of either defending the truth or refuting falsehood? That those, to move and force the minds of their hearers into error, should be able by their style to terrify them, move them to tears, make them laugh, give them rousing encouragement, while these on behalf of truth stumble along slow, cold and half asleep?"

# THE ETHICS OF PERSUASION

R EFER BACK TO THIS ETHICAL GUIDE as needed. I created this in a spirit of humility, for my benefit as much as for the benefit of my readers. And you don't have to choose between efficacy and ethics. When I followed these principles, my words became more ethical *and* more powerful.

FOLLOW THESE TWELVE RULES. Do not use false, fabricated, misrepresented, distorted, or irrelevant evidence to support claims. Do not intentionally use specious, unsupported, or illogical reasoning. Do not represent yourself as informed or as an "expert" on a subject when you are not. Do not use irrelevant appeals to divert attention from the issue at hand. Do not cause intense but unreflective emotional reactions. Do not link your idea to emotion-laden values, motives, or goals to which it is not related. Do not hide your real purpose or self-interest, the group you represent, or your position as an advocate of a viewpoint. Do not distort, hide, or misrepresent the number, scope, or intensity of bad effects. Do not use emotional appeals that lack a basis of evidence or reasoning or that would fail if the audience examined the subject themselves. Do not oversimplify complex, gradation-laden situations into simplistic two-valued, either/or, polar views or choices. Do not pretend certainty where tentativeness and degrees of probability would be more accurate. Do not advocate something you do not believe (Johannesen et al., 2021).

APPLY THIS GOLDEN HEURISTIC. In a 500,000-word book, you might be able to tell your audience everything you know about a subject. In a five-minute persuasive speech, you can only select a small sampling of your knowledge. Would learning your entire body of knowledge result in a significantly different reaction than hearing the small sampling you selected? If the answer is yes, that's a problem.

SWING WITH THE GOOD EDGE. Rhetoric is a double-edged sword. It can express good ideas well. It can also express bad ideas well. Rhetoric makes ideas attractive; tempting; credible; persuasive. Don't use it to turn weakly-worded lies into well-worded lies. Use it to turn weakly-worded truths into well-worded truths.

TREAT TRUTH AS THE HIGHEST GOOD. Use any persuasive strategy, unless using it in your circumstances would distort the truth. The strategies should not come between you and truth, or compromise your honesty and authenticity.

AVOID THE SPIRIT OF DECEIT. Wrong statements are incorrect statements you genuinely believe. Lies are statements you know are wrong but convey anyway. Deceitful statements are not literally wrong, but you convey them with the intent to mislead, obscure, hide, or manipulate. Hiding relevant information is not literally lying (saying you conveyed all the information would be). Cherry-picking facts is not literally lying (saying there are no other facts would be). Using clever innuendo to twist reality without making any concrete claims is not literally lying (knowingly making a false accusation would be). And yet, these are all examples of deceit. ONLY USE STRATEGIES IF THEY ARE ACCURATE. Motivate unified thinking. Inspire loving thinking. These strategies sound good. Use the victim-perpetrator-benevolence structure. Paint a common enemy. Appeal to tribal psychology. These strategies sound bad. But when reality lines up with the strategies that sound bad, they become good. They are only bad when they are inaccurate or move people down a bad path. *But the same is true for the ones that sound good.* Should Winston Churchill have motivated unified thinking? Not toward his enemy. Should he have avoided appealing to tribal psychology to strengthen the Allied war effort? Should he have avoided painting a common enemy? Should he have avoided portraying the victimization of true victims and the perpetration of a true perpetrator? Should he have avoided calling people to act as the benevolent force for good, protecting the victim and beating back the perpetrator? Don't use the victim-perpetrator-benevolence structure if there aren't clear victims and perpetrators. This is demagoguery. Painting false victims disempowers them. But if there are true victims and perpetrators, stand up for the victims and stand against the perpetrators, calling others to join you as a benevolent force for justice. Don't motivate unified thinking when standing against evil. Don't hold back from portraying a common enemy when there is one. Some strategies might sound morally suspect. Some might sound inherently good. But it depends on the situation. Every time I say "do X to achieve Y," remember the condition: "if it is accurate and moves people up a good path."

APPLY THE TARES TEST: truthfulness of message, authenticity of persuader, respect for audience, equity of persuasive appeal, and social impact (TARES).

REMEMBER THE THREE-PART VENN DIAGRAM: words that are authentic, effective, and true. Donald Miller once said "I'm the kind of person who wants to present my most honest, authentic self to the world, so I hide backstage and rehearse honest and authentic lines until the curtain opens." There's nothing dishonest or inauthentic about choosing your words carefully and making them more effective, as long as they remain just as true. Rhetoric takes a messy marble brick of truth and sculpts it into a poised, precise, and perfect statue. It takes weak truths and makes them strong. Unfortunately, it can do the same for weak lies. But preparing, strategizing, and sculpting is not inauthentic. Unskillfulness is no more authentic than skillfulness. Unpreparedness is no more authentic than preparedness.

APPLY FITZPATRICK AND GAUTHIER'S THREE-QUESTION ANALYSIS. For what purpose is persuasion being employed? Toward what choices and with what consequences for individual lives is it being used? Does the persuasion contribute to or interfere with the audience's decision-making process (Lumen, 2016)?

**STRENGTHEN THE TRUTH.** Rhetoric makes words strong. Use it to turn truths strong, not falsities strong. There are four categories of language: weak and wrong, strong and wrong, weak and true, strong and true. Turn weak and true language into strong and true language. Don't turn weak and wrong language into strong and wrong language, weak and true language into strong and wrong language, or strong and true language into weak and true language. Research. Question your assumptions. Strive for truth. Ensure your logic is impeccable. Defuse your biases.

**START WITH FINDING TRUTH.** The rhetorical endeavor starts with becoming as knowledgeable on your subject as possible and developing an impeccable logical argument. The more research you do, the more rhetoric you earn the right to use.

**PUT TRUTH BEFORE STYLE.** Rhetorical skill does not make you correct. Truth doesn't care about your rhetoric. If your rhetoric is brilliant, but you realize your arguments are simplistic, flawed, or biased, change course. Let logic lead style. Don't sacrifice logic to style. Don't express bad ideas well. Distinguish effective speaking from effective rational argument. Achieve both, but put reason and logic first.

**AVOID THE POPULARITY VORTEX.** As Plato suggested, avoid "giving the citizens what they want [in speech] with no thought to whether they will be better or worse as a result of what you are saying." Ignore the temptation to gain positive reinforcement and instant gratification from the audience with no merit to your message. Rhetoric is unethical if used solely to appeal rather than to help the world.

**CONSIDER THE CONSEQUENCES.** If you succeed to persuade people, will the world become better or worse? Will your audience benefit? Will you benefit? Moreover, is it the best action they could take? Or would an alternative help more? Is it an objectively worthwhile investment? Is it the best solution? Are you giving them all the facts they need to determine this on their own?

**CONSIDER SECOND- AND THIRD-ORDER IMPACTS.** Consider not only immediate consequences, but consequences across time. Consider the impact of the action you seek to persuade, as well as the tools you use to persuade it. Maybe the action is objectively positive, but in motivating the action, you resorted to instilling beliefs that will cause damage over time. Consider their long-term impact as well.

**KNOW THAT BAD ACTORS ARE PLAYING THE SAME GAME.** Bad actors already know how to be persuasive and how to spread their lies. They already know the tools. And many lies are more tempting than truth and easier to believe by their very nature. Truth waits for us to find it at the bottom of a muddy well. Truth is complicated, and complexity is harder to convey with impact. Use these tools to give truth a fighting chance in an arena where bad actors have a natural advantage. Use your knowledge to counter and defuse these tools when people misuse them.

**APPLY THE FIVE ETHICAL APPROACHES:** seek the greatest good for the greatest number (utilitarian); protect the rights of those affected and treat people not as means but as ends (rights); treat equals equally and nonequals fairly (justice); set the good of humanity as the basis of your moral reasoning (common good); act consistently with the ideals that lead to your self-actualization and the highest potential of your character (virtue). Say and do what is right, not what is expedient, and be willing to suffer the consequences of doing so. Don't place self-gratification, acquisitiveness, social status, and power over the common good of all humanity.

APPLY THE FOUR ETHICAL DECISION-MAKING CRITERIA: respect for individual rights to make choices, hold views, and act based on personal beliefs and values (autonomy); the maximization of benefits and the minimization of harms, acting for the benefit of others, helping others further their legitimate interests; taking action to prevent or remove possible harms (beneficence); acting in ways that cause no harm, avoid the risk of harm, and assuring benefits outweigh costs (non-maleficence); treating others according to a defensible standard (justice).

USE ILLOGICAL PROCESSES TO GET ETHICAL RESULTS. Using flawed thinking processes to get good outcomes is not unethical. Someone who disagrees should stop speaking with conviction, clarity, authority, and effective paralanguage. All are irrelevant to the truth of their words, but impact the final judgment of the audience. You must use logic and evidence to figure out the truth. But this doesn't mean logic and evidence will persuade others. Humans have two broad categories of cognitive functions: system one is intuitive, emotional, fast, heuristic-driven, and generally illogical; system two is rational, deliberate, evidence-driven, and generally logical. The best-case scenario is to get people to believe right things for right reasons (through system two). The next best case is to get people to believe right things for wrong reasons (through system one). Both are far better than letting people believe wrong things for wrong reasons. If you don't use those processes, they still function, but lead people astray. You can reverse-engineer them. If you know the truth, have an abundance of reasons to be confident you know the truth, and can predict the disasters that will occur if people don't believe the truth, don't you have a responsibility to be as effective as possible in bringing people to the truth? Logic and evidence are essential, of course. They will persuade many. They should have persuaded you. But people can't always follow a long chain of reasoning or a complicated argument. Persuade by eloquence what you learned by reason.

HELP YOUR SELF-INTEREST. (But not at the expense of your audience or without their knowledge). Ethics calls for improving the world, and you are a part of the world – the one you control most. Improving yourself is a service to others.

APPLY THE WINDOWPANE STANDARD. In Aristotle's view, rhetoric reveals how to persuade and how to defeat manipulative persuaders. Thus, top students of rhetoric would be master speakers, trained to anticipate and disarm the rhetorical tactics of their adversaries. According to this tradition, language is only useful to the extent that it does not distort reality, and good writing functions as a "windowpane," helping people peer through the wall of ignorance and view reality. You might think this precludes persuasion. You might think this calls for dry academic language. But what good is a windowpane if nobody cares to look through it? What good is a windowpane to reality if, on the other wall, a stained-glass window distorts reality but draws people to it? The best windowpane reveals as much of reality as possible while drawing as many people to it as possible. RUN THROUGH THESE INTROSPECTIVE QUESTIONS. Are the means truly unethical or merely distasteful, unpopular, or unwise? Is the end truly good, or does it simply appear good because we desire it? Is it probable that bad means will achieve the good end? Is the same good achievable using more ethical means if we are creative, patient, and skillful? Is the good end clearly and overwhelmingly better than any bad effects of the means used to attain it? Will the use of unethical means to achieve a good end withstand public scrutiny? Could the use of unethical means be justified to those most affected and those most impartial? Can I specify my ethical criteria or standards? What is the grounding of the ethical judgment? Can I justify the reasonableness and relevancy of these standards for this case? Why are these the best criteria? Why do they take priority? How does the communication succeed or fail by these standards? What judgment is justified in this case about the degree of ethicality? Is it a narrowly focused one rather than a broad and generalized one? To whom is ethical responsibility owed – to which individuals, groups, organizations, or professions? In what ways and to what extent? Which take precedence? What is my responsibility to myself and society? How do I feel about myself after this choice? Can I continue to "live with myself?" Would I want my family to know of this choice? Does the choice reflect my ethical character? To what degree is it "out of character?" If called upon in public to justify the ethics of my communication, how adequately could I do so? What generally accepted reasons could I offer? Are there precedents which can guide me? Are there aspects of this case that set it apart from others? How thoroughly have alternatives been explored before settling on this choice? Is it less ethical than some of the workable alternatives? If the goal requires unethical communication, can I abandon the goal (Johannesen et al., 2007)?

VIEW YOURSELF AS A GUIDE. Stories have a hero, a villain who stands in his way, and a guide who helps the hero fulfill his mission. If you speak ineffectively, you are a nonfactor. If you speak deceitfully, you become the villain. But if you convey truth effectively, you become the guide in your audience's story, who leads them, teaches them, inspires them, and helps them overcome adversity and win. Use your words to put people on the best possible path. And if you hide an ugly truth, ask yourself this: "If I found out that *my* guide omitted this, how would I react?"

APPLY THE PUZZLE ANALOGY. Think of rhetoric as a piece in the puzzle of reality. Only use a rhetorical approach if it fits with the most logical, rational, and evidence-based view of reality. If it doesn't, it's the wrong puzzle piece. Try another.

KNOW THAT THE TRUTH WILL OUT. The truth can either come out in your words, or you can deceive people. You can convince them to live in a fantasy. And that might work. Until. Until truth breaks down the door and storms the building. Until the facade comes crashing down and chaos makes its entry. Slay the dragon in its lair before it comes to your village. Invite truth in through the front door before truth burns the building down. Truth wins in the end, either because a good person spreads, defends, and fights for it, or because untruth reveals itself as such by its consequences, and does so in brutal and painful fashion, hurting innocents and perpetrators alike. Trust and reputation take years to create and seconds to destroy. MAXIMIZE THE TWO HIERARCHIES OF SUCCESS: honesty *and* effectiveness. You could say "Um, well, uh, I think that um, what we should… should uh… do, is that, well… let me think… er, I think if we are more, you know… fluid, we'll be better at… producing, I mean, progressing, and producing, and just more generally, you know, getting better results, but… I guess my point is, like, that, that if we are more fluid and do things more better, we will get better results than with a bureaucracy and, you know how it is, a silo-based structure, right? I mean… you know what I mean." Or, you could say "Bravery beats bureaucracy, courage beats the status quo, and innovation beats stagnation." Is one of those statements truer? No. Is one of them more effective? Is one of them more likely to get positive action that instantiates the truth into the world? Yes. Language is not reality. It provides signposts to reality. Two different signposts can point at the same truth – they can be equally and maximally true – and yet one can be much more effective. One gets people to follow the road. One doesn't. Maximize honesty. Then, insofar as it doesn't sacrifice honesty, maximize effectiveness. Speak truth. And speak it well.

KNOW THAT DECEPTION SINKS THE SHIP. Deception prevents perception. If someone deceives everyone onboard a ship, blinding them in a sense, they may get away with self-serving behavior. But eventually, they get hurt by the fate they designed. The ship sinks. How could it not? The waters are hazardous. If the crew is operating with distorted perceptions, they fail to see the impending dangers in the deep. So it is with teams, organizations, and entire societies.

APPLY THE WISDOM OF THIS QUOTE. Mary Beard, an American historian, author, and activist, captured the essence of ethical rhetoric well: "What politicians do is they never get the rhetoric wrong, and the price they pay is they don't speak the truth as they see it. Now, I will speak truth as I see it, and sometimes I don't get the rhetoric right. I think that's a fair trade-off." It's more than fair. It's necessary.

REMEMBER YOUR RESPONSIBILITY TO SOCIETY. Be a guardian of the truth. Speak out against wrongdoing, and do it well. The solution to evil speech is not less speech, but more (good) speech. Create order with your words, not chaos. Our civilization depends on it. Match the truth, honesty, and vulnerable transparency of your words against the irreducible complexity of the universe. And in this complex universe, remember the omnipresence of nuance, and the dangers of simplistic ideologies. (Inconveniently, simplistic ideologies are persuasive, while nuanced truths are difficult to convey. This is why good people need to be verbally skilled; to pull the extra weight of conveying a realistic worldview). Don't commit your whole mind to an isolated fragment of truth, lacking context, lacking nuance. Be precise in your speech, to ensure you are saying what you mean to say. Memorize the logical fallacies, the cognitive biases, and the rules of logic and correct thinking. (Conveniently, many rhetorical devices are also reasoning devices that focus your inquiry and help you explicate truth). But don't demonize those with good intentions and bad ideas. If they are forthcoming and honest, they are not your enemy. Rather, the two of you are on a shared mission to find the truth, partaking in a shared commitment to reason and dialogue. The malevolent enemy doesn't care about the truth. And in this complex world, remember Voltaire's warning to "cherish those who seek the truth but beware of those who find it," and Aristotle's startling observation that "the least deviation from truth [at the start] is multiplied a thousandfold." Be cautious in determining what to say with conviction. Good speaking is not a substitute for good thinking. The danger zone is being confidently incorrect. What hurts us most is what we know that just isn't so. Remember these tenets and your responsibility, and rhetoric becomes the irreplaceable aid of the good person doing good things in difficult times; the sword of the warrior of the light.

KNOW THAT DECEPTION IS ITS OWN PUNISHMENT. Knowingly uttering a falsehood is a spoken lie of commission. Having something to say but not saying it is a spoken lie of omission. Knowingly behaving inauthentically is an acted-out lie of commission. Knowingly omitting authentic behavior is an acted-out lie of omission. All these deceptions weaken your being. All these deceptions corrupt your own mind, turning your greatest asset into an ever-present companion you can no longer trust. Your conscience operates somewhat autonomously, and it will call you out (unless your repeated neglect desensitizes it). You have a conscious conscience which speaks clearly, and an unconscious conscience, which communicates more subtly. A friend of mine asked: "Why do we feel relieved when we speak truth? Why are we drawn toward it, even if it is not pleasant? Do our brains have something that makes this happen?" Yes, they do: our consciences, our inner lights, our inner north stars. And we feel relieved because living with the knowledge of our own deceit is often an unbearable burden. You live your life before an audience of one: yourself. You cannot escape the observation of your own awareness; you can't hide from yourself. Everywhere you go, there you are. Everything you do, there you are. Some of the greatest heights of wellbeing come from performing well in this one-man theater, and signaling virtue to yourself; being someone you are proud to be (and grateful to observe). Every time you lie, you tell your subconscious mind that your character is too weak to contend with the truth. And this shapes your character accordingly. It becomes true. And then what? Lying carries its own punishment, even if the only person who catches the liar is the liar himself.

BE A MONSTER (THEN LEARN TO CONTROL IT). There is nothing moral about weakness and harmlessness. The world is difficult. There are threats to confront, oppressors to resist, and tyrants to rebuff. (Peterson, 2018). There are psychopaths, sociopaths, and Machiavellian actors with no love for the common good. There is genuine malevolence. If you are incapable of being an effective deceiver, then you are incapable of being an effective advocate for truth: it is the same weapon, pointed in different directions. If you cannot use it in both directions, can you use it at all? Become a monster, become dangerous, and become capable of convincing people to believe in a lie... and then use this ability to convince them to believe in the truth. The capacity for harm is also the capacity for harming harmful entities; that is to say, defending innocent ones. If you can't hurt anyone, you can't help anyone when they need someone to stand up for them. Words are truly weapons, and the most powerful weapons in the world at that. The ability to use them, for good *or* for bad, is the prerequisite to using them for good. There is an archetype in our cultural narratives: the well-intentioned but harmless protagonist who gets roundly defeated by the villain, until he develops his monstrous edge and integrates it, at which point he becomes the triumphant hero. Along similar lines, I watched a film about an existential threat to humanity, in which the protagonist sought to convey the threat to a skeptical public, but failed miserably because he lacked the rhetorical skill to do so. The result? The world ended. Everyone died. The protagonist was of no use to anyone. And this almost became a true story. A historical study showed that in the Cuban Missile Crisis, the arguments that won out in the United States mastermind group were not the best, but those argued with the most conviction. Those with the best arguments lacked the skill to match. The world (could have) ended. The moral? Speak truth... well.

## MASTERING COMMUNICATION, ONE SKILL AT A TIME

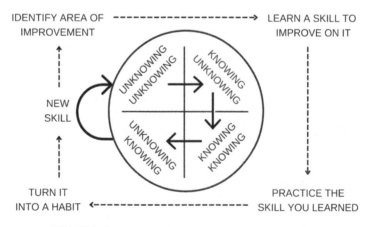

FIGURE I: The proven path to mastery.

**effective**

...............................................................................

*adjective*

    successful in producing a desired or intended result

**communication**

...............................................................................

*noun*

    the imparting or exchanging of information or news

# CONTENTS

# THE MIDDLE: 165

# BEFORE YOU GO...

Rhetoric, Motivated by Love, Guided by Reason, and Aimed at Truth, Is a Powerful Force for the Greatest Good.

## POLITICAL DISCLAIMER

Throughout this book, and throughout all my books, I draw examples of communication strategies from the political world. I quote from the speeches of many of America's great leaders, like JFK and MLK, as well as from more recent political figures of both major parties. Political communication is ideal for illustrating the concepts revealed in the books. It is the best source of examples of words that work that I have ever found. I don't use anything out of the political mainstream. And it is by extensively studying the inaugural addresses of United States Presidents and the great speeches of history that I have discovered many of the speaking strategies I share with you.

My using the words of any particular figure to illustrate a principle of communication is not necessarily an endorsement of the figure or their message. Separate the speaker from the strategy. After all, the strategy is the only reason the speaker made an appearance in the book at all. Would you rather have a weak example of a strategy you want to learn from a speaker you love, or a perfect example of the strategy from a speaker you detest?

For a time, I didn't think a disclaimer like this was necessary. I thought people would do this on their own. I thought that if people read an example of a strategy drawn from the words of a political figure they disagreed with, they would appreciate the value of the example as an instructive tool and set aside their negative feelings about the speaker. "Yes, I don't agree with this speaker or the message, but I can clearly see the strategy in this example and I now have a better understanding of how it works and how to execute it." Indeed, I suspect 95% of my readers do just that. You probably will, too. But if you are part of the 5% who aren't up for it, don't say I didn't warn you, and please don't leave a negative review because you think I endorse this person or that person. I don't, as this is strictly a book about communication.

# THE

# PSYCHOLOGY

# OF

# COMMUNICATION

### THE UNDERGROUND GUIDE TO PERSUASIVE
### PRESENTATIONS AND EASY ELOQUENCE

**SPEAK FOR SUCCESS COLLECTION BOOK**

# XIV

**THE PSYCHOLOGY OF COMMUNICATION CHAPTER**

# I

# MAGNETIC PRESENCE:

## How to Own the Room and Captivate Attention

## I COULDN'T TALK – AND THEN I COULD...

P UBLIC SPEAKING ANXIETY USED TO cripple me. Before every speech, presentation, meeting, debate, discussion – whatever it was – I would shake and envision failure. No matter how well I ended up doing, I always felt like the nerves were holding me back. And more often than not, I did not do well at all: stutters, stumbles, and self-evident nerves plagued my speech.

I knew I wanted to master the skill. I knew it would be essential to my later success (and this was proven correct, albeit in a more immediate way than I could have imagined). But I knew I was not in a good starting place. I was by no means a natural.

What did I do? Practice. Practice. Practice.

Did I get better? No, but I kept going. Practice. Practice. Practice.

I started competing in debates. I would practice by pulling up the news, picking a headline, reading an article, and immediately giving a five-minute speech in rebuttal to the article. I started voraciously consuming the speeches of legendary leaders throughout history, studying them the way a psychologist studies a patient; digging for their hidden secrets of rhetoric like an archeologist looking for an ancient artifact. I picked up books on rhetoric, psychology, and building self-confidence. I was fully devoted to this pursuit. I would master the art, I told myself. I now realize this was a misguided quest: the nature of the art is that it cannot be mastered. It can only be improved upon. Regardless, I progressed. Slowly at first, then fast.

Fast forward a few years. My competitive public speaking career came to a close. Allow me to share my "career statistics" so you can decide if you trust me to teach you this skill or not.

I was the state champion in my category. I gave about 300-400 speeches – some in front of audiences of 200 people – and loved every second of it. I won eight state-wide tournaments, in the state with the most competitive circuits. I won national competitions. I received a seal of special distinction, and apparently left behind an unparalleled competitive record in the ~50 year history of the league (I never bothered to check – someone else told me).

When my competitive career ended, I decided to make a business of teaching others the skill I had learned. I since wrote 22 books on public speaking, effective communication, and persuasion, with about half of them enjoying best-seller status at one point in time. I heard from countless readers who came close to mastering the skill after reading my work. I personally coached 300 mentees, including one of the country's top project managers, a Toastmasters national finalist, and a candidate for political office. I read thousands of speeches and hundreds of scientific studies on psychology, each revealing more secrets of effective communication to me.

I don't say this to brag (although I do enjoy bragging). I say it so you know who you're learning from, so you can make an informed decision about whether you trust my experience. I also say it so you know the background from which the central idea of this book emerged. And what's that central idea? Presence.

## WHAT IS PRESENCE?

The best way to explain it is with a story. In some form, this story has repeated itself time and again over the course of my competitive public speaking career.

Imagine a room with 30 people practicing speeches in it, minutes before a competition. Loud, right? Imagine 29 of them suddenly stopping. One moment, the room is filled with a cacophony of voices, all wrapped up in their own little worlds, and in another moment, they are all fiercely tuned in on one voice. That would be me. Did I yell? Did I say "may I have your attention please?" or "excuse me – I have an announcement to make!" Nope. I was just delivering my speech. But the combination of content and delivery gave me a magnetic presence that grabbed practically everyone's attention, practically instantly.

Imagine another scenario: You are debating someone who keeps winning debates, and you don't particularly like him. I am the that person in this scenario. Your one purpose is to eliminate him from the competition, revealing the absurdity of his ideas, demolishing his foolish perspective, and embarrassing him in front of the audience. You mean to interject, cutting him off at a crucial juncture of his argument, stating your rebuttal in forceful terms. But for some reason, you keep forgetting what you wanted to say. You keep listening to him. You keep getting wrapped up in his message. You can't seem to pull your attention away for even a moment to formulate your rebuttal – he keeps grabbing it back, like a magnet.

---

**KEY INSIGHT:**

Presence Is Magnetism, And Magnetism Is Presence. Attention Magnetism, To Be Precise.

Certain Speaking Patterns Create Presence. They Captivate Attention, Quickly and Easily.

---

## THESE STRATEGIES WILL TURN YOU INTO A MAGNET

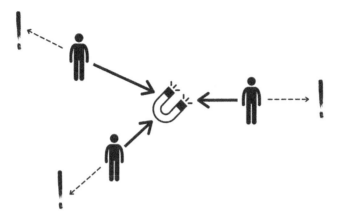

FIGURE 1: These proven, step-by-step speaking strategies appeal to the fundamental psychology of attention. As a result, you will almost always win out over competing "distracting" inputs. You will be a magnet.

Now, these stories didn't just happen to me – they happened to those I taught as well, time and time again. What do these stories have to do with this book? I will explain...

## YOUR FOUR LANGUAGES

You have four languages. You are quadlingual. You speak four languages fluently – or semi-fluently. "Bilingual" people, in the traditional sense of the word, speak five languages. "Trilingual" people speak six.

What are your four languages? You have your "language language," which is probably English. You have your body language. You have your verbal language (that is how your voice sounds when you say what you say). You have, occasionally, your visual language: slides or other visual aids you present to your audience. And, if you are "bilingual," you have a fifth language: your second "language language." Mine is Romanian. I speak five languages.

Understanding this is one of the essential paradigm shifts that will drastically improve your communication, simply by grasping it intellectually.

What is magnetic presence? It is patterns of these four languages (or three, as visual aid are not always in play), producing a gravitational pull toward you that is almost irresistible. People will stop their own conversations and listen to you. People who want to destroy your ideas will often not be able to, simply for the reason that they can't stop listening to you explain your ideas.

### HOW TO MASTER THE FOUR LEVELS OF COMMUNICATION

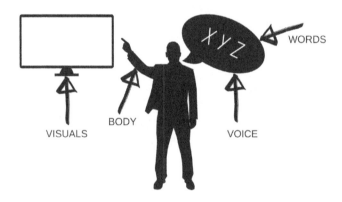

FIGURE 2: You speak with four languages: words, voice, body language, and visuals. This book deals primarily with maximizing the impact of your word language.

### THE SPEAKING PATTERNS

This book focuses on strategies producing magnetic presence that fall into the "language language" bucket: specific sequences of strategically selected words you can use to achieve magnetic presence. It reveals 211 of these speaking patterns. It reveals patterns for grabbing attention (openings), patterns and strategies for keeping attention (transitions), and patterns for channeling attention toward a definite purpose (endings).

**HOW TO GRAB, KEEP, AND DIRECT ATTENTION**

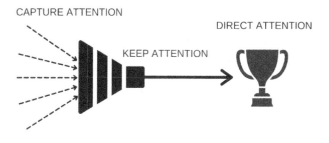

FIGURE 3: This book breaks down into a three-part framework: opening strategies for capturing attention, transitioning strategies for keeping attention, and closing strategies for directing attention to a worthy purpose.

## THIS IS THE BEST PART

I am a public speaker at heart. That's my background. But the best part of this secret is that it works with all types of communication. Writing, speaking to one person, *anything*. I want you to remember this as we go on: *if it's communication, these strategies work.* The reason I tell you this now is because I portray these ideas through the lens of giving a presentation or a speech, and sometimes speaking to a single person. But the scope of these ideas is limitless. They directly translate to writing too, for example. You can use these to help make the words on the website you manage for your company more impactful, captivating, and persuasive. You can use these to craft mor engaging subject lines for customer-facing emails. You can use these principles to determine why some products capture an audience while others are ignored. They are broad-based principles with sweeping implications. You'll see for yourself. Ask yourself: "How would I use this in an email? In a product description? In a report? In a whitepaper?"

### ALL COMMUNICATION IS FUNDAMENTALLY THE SAME

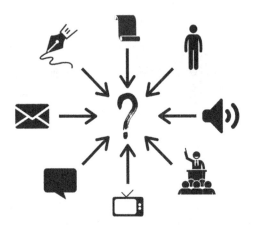

FIGURE 4: These strategies work in all types of communication. Beyond the superficial differences, all communication is fundamentally the same.

.................................Chapter Summary................................

- Presence is when people can't help tuning in, giving you their complete and undivided attention.
- Proven, predictable, step-by-step speaking patterns achieve presence by appealing to human psychology.
- These speaking patterns grab attention, hold attention, and then direct attention to a worthy purpose.
- This book is a manual, revealing over 200 of these proven speaking patterns. You can use them in writing as well.
- You speak with four languages: your vocal language, your body language, your word language, and your visuals.

- This book helps you perfect your word language, ensuring that what you say achieves impact and engages people.

---

**KEY INSIGHT:**

The Medium Is Relatively Superficial And, In Some Cases, Even Irrelevant.

No Matter the Surface Medium, There Is An Underlying Medium: Human Connection.

This Medium, This True Medium, Is Always the Same.

---

Email Peter D. Andrei, the author of the Speak for Success collection and the President of Speak Truth Well LLC directly.

pandreibusiness@gmail.com

## THREE PHRASES, THREE STEPS, THREE PARTS OF A WHOLE, COMPLETING EACH OTHER

### BEGINNING

Grab attention, create tension, generate interest, raise curiosity...

### MIDDLE

Use evidence, logic, and noble emotional appeals to generate motivation and drive...

### END

Direct that motivation and drive toward a clear and specific action...

Claim These Free Resources that Will Help You Unleash the Power of Your Words and Speak with Confidence. Visit www.speakforsuccesshub.com/toolkit for Access.

### 18 Free PDF Resources

*12 Iron Rules for Captivating Story, 21 Speeches that Changed the World, 341-Point Influence Checklist, 143 Persuasive Cognitive Biases, 17 Ways to Think On Your Feet, 18 Lies About Speaking Well, 137 Deadly Logical Fallacies, 12 Iron Rules For Captivating Slides, 371 Words that Persuade, 63 Truths of Speaking Well, 27 Laws of Empathy, 21 Secrets of Legendary Speeches, 19 Scripts that Persuade, 12 Iron Rules For Captivating Speech, 33 Laws of Charisma, 11 Influence Formulas, 219-Point Speech-Writing Checklist, 21 Eloquence Formulas*

**Claim These Free Resources that Will Help You Unleash the Power of Your Words and Speak with Confidence. Visit www.speakforsuccesshub.com/toolkit for Access.**

**30 Free Video Lessons**

We'll send you one free video lesson every day for 30 days, written and recorded by Peter D. Andrei. Days 1-10 cover authenticity, the prerequisite to confidence and persuasive power. Days 11-20 cover building self-belief and defeating communication anxiety. Days 21-30 cover how to speak with impact and influence, ensuring your words change minds instead of falling flat. Authenticity, self-belief, and impact – this course helps you master three components of confidence, turning even the most high-stakes presentations from obstacles into opportunities.

**Claim These Free Resources that Will Help You Unleash the Power of Your Words and Speak with Confidence. Visit www.speakforsuccesshub.com/toolkit for Access.**

**2 Free Workbooks**

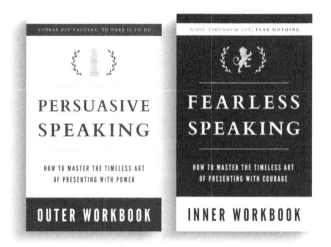

We'll send you two free workbooks, including long-lost excerpts by Dale Carnegie, the mega-bestselling author of *How to Win Friends and Influence People* (5,000,000 copies sold). *Fearless Speaking* guides you in the proven principles of mastering your inner game as a speaker. *Persuasive Speaking* guides you in the time-tested tactics of mastering your outer game by maximizing the power of your words. All of these resources complement the Speak for Success collection.

SPEAK FOR SUCCESS COLLECTION BOOK

# XIV

THE PSYCHOLOGY OF COMMUNICATION CHAPTER

# II

# THE BEGINNING:
## Grabbing Attention

## HOW TO START YOUR COMMUNICATION THE RIGHT WAY

C HANCES ARE YOU DON'T KNOW THE BASICS of how to start a speech. Most people don't. And that will make public speaking much scarier. If you don't start right, you probably won't finish right. And if you don't start right, you likely won't achieve magnetic presence.

### WHY IT'S SO IMPORTANT

If you don't get your audience's attention at the start, you may never get it. If you don't start well, you won't speak well, and you certainly won't finish well. I can often tell if a speech will be good or bad based on the first 15 seconds. A good opening almost always means a good speech. But a bad opening? A weak speech almost always follows.

**THE OPENING OFTEN DETERMINES THE ENDING**

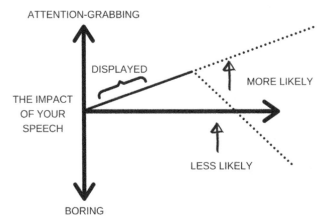

FIGURE 5: If a speaker displays attention-grabbing and engaging speech at the beginning, continuing successfully is much more likely than beginning to falter. The reverse applies as well.

## IT ONLY GETS HARDER FROM THE START

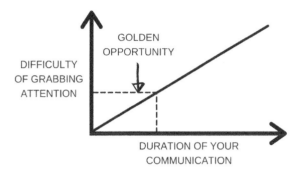

FIGURE 6: It only gets more difficult to grab attention as the speech progresses. As the duration of your communication extend, the difficulty of grabbing attention rises. The start of your speech acts as a moment of golden opportunity, when it is easiest to grab attention. Take advantage of this moment with the proven openings.

## PRESENTING A MORE NUANCED ATTENTION DISTRIBUTION

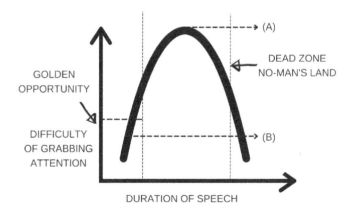

FIGURE 7: The previous figure left out some nuance. It is more accurate to say that the difficulty of grabbing attention acts as a bell curve. At the beginning of a speech, it is the easiest to grab attention. Likewise, at the end, it is roughly

as easy as it was at the beginning. Throughout the middle, the difficulty tends to rise. Take advantage of the golden opportunity at the beginning. Make sure you have attained attention by the time you get into the dead zone. Grabbing attention in the middle is both significantly harder and less valuable, as you only keep it for half of the speech (A). If you grab it at the golden opportunity – which is easier – and if you don't lose it, you keep it throughout the entire speech (B). At the start, they are fresh slates. Toward the end, they perceive the conclusion of the speech and tune in again. This is a theoretical model: Specifics may vary.

## PERSONAL INTROS

You absolutely *should* introduce yourself when you speak. But that introduction absolutely *should not* happen before your speech opening. In other words: your speech opening is not your personal introduction. Why? *People don't care about you.* Sorry. They care about themselves. And they need to hear a strong speech opening before they decide to listen to you talk about yourself. So, to fix this mistake, read the next step.

### WHAT ARE PEOPLE CONSTANTLY THINKING?

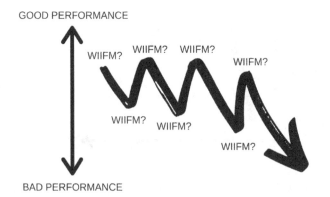

FIGURE 8: You may feel that as you make mistakes or perform well, your audience shifts their internal monologue

accordingly. You might think they are thinking "wow, what a great speaker!" when you are performing well, and "ouch, that was awkward" when you make a mistake. On some level, this might be true. But underlying most people's internal mental dialogue most of the time is the question of "what's in it for me?" or "WIIFM?"

## FOLLOW THE PROPER ORDER OF AFFAIRS

Most speakers do something like this. Personal introduction: "Here's who I am! I went to this school, studied this, and now I work as an aide to the president." Speech opening: "Today, we're going to talk about a threat to our nation." And then the speech. Not bad. But if you're wondering how to start a speech, that is not how. Instead, do this. Speech opening: "Today, we're going to talk about a threat to our nation." Personal introduction: "Here's who I am! I went to this school, studied this, and now I work as an aide to the president." And then the rest of the speech.

What's more captivating? The "threat to our nation" statement? Or the "here's who I am" statement? Definitely the threat statement. And it is so captivating that it can even hold people's attention while you describe yourself.

It can become even better. How? By molding the personal introduction and the speech opening together. The fact that the speaker is an aide to the president is only important in the context of the subject: a threat to the nation. So, a better option is this: Speech opening / personal intro: "Today, we're going to talk about a threat to our nation that I noticed in my work as an aide to the president." More speech opening / personal intro: "I couldn't conceive of anything like this threat when I was studying international relations at [insert school]. But here it is, happening anyway." And then the rest of the speech. See how that's more captivating? It sneaks personal information (which is important) among opening material (which is *more* important). Why is this necessary? Information foraging.

## HOW TO START WITH MAXIMUM ENGAGEMENT

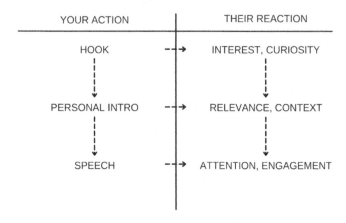

FIGURE 9: This is the proper order of affairs for ensuring you grab attention in the golden opportunity. The hook creates interest and curiosity. After the hook, the personal introduction presents relevance and context. Then, you enjoy attention and engagement during the speech.

## INFORMATION FORAGING

People forage for information the same way animals forage for food. They go from patch to patch, testing before committing. In the information age, this is magnified, because a more promising patch always seems to be around the corner, and reaching it has the low cost of a few clicks. And when they are sitting there with you in front of them, they go through a checklist, often subconsciously and often extremely quickly. This checklist typically includes things like: "Does this message have anything to do with me? Will it help me survive or thrive? Is the speaker going to waste my attention, or minimize the amount of attention and concentration and interpretation I need to force upon my lazy mind to get the message?" Your message passes? Great, they listen. It doesn't pass? You lose them, and have a harder time getting them back later on. They are bombarded with information. They can't possibly take it all in, so they use a mental, subconscious, quick checklist to filter information.

Do you think where you went to school passes their checklist? No. How about that you work as a personal aide to the president? Maybe. Do you think the major threat to our nation and our American way of life passes their checklist? Yes. Absolutely.

You might be thinking "if I'm going to be talking about the major threat anyway, why does any of this matter?" Because they go through the checklist at the *beginning*. They use the checklist when you start, to determine if they should mentally engage. So, it doesn't matter what your content is overall, it matters what you're saying at the exact moment they are going through the mental checklist. That's why speech openings are so important, and why you must maximize information scent...

### THIS IS HOW PEOPLE DECIDE TO PAY ATTENTION

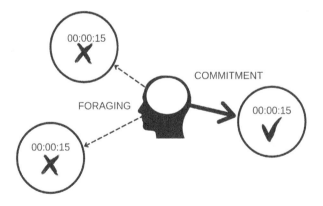

FIGURE 10: This is how people decide to pay attention. This visualizes the information foraging dynamic. They will test one patch of information for 15 seconds to determine its "information scent." Based on this, they will commit or reject it. Then, they will move on to patch after patch, until they find one that passes the 15-second information scent test. Then, they will commit to this.

## MAXIMIZE INFORMATION SCENT

Pack the most attention–grabbing, interesting, powerful content in your opening. Why? Because that's what passes their "relevant information" checklist. In the world of information foraging theory, that's called information scent. It's how people determine if something passes their mental checklist before committing to it.

### WHAT DO THESE STRATEGIES DO TO GRAB ATTENTION?

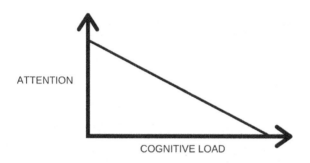

FIGURE 11: These strategies, in addition to raising information scent directly (by raising perceived gain of information), also raise it indirectly by lowering cognitive load (by lowering perceived cost of information). As cognitive load rises, attention drops.

## CRISP, COMMANDING PHRASES

Short. Punchy. Crisp. Commanding. That's what you want. These sentences are no-nonsense. These sentences demand attention and generate respect. These sentences draw people in. In your opening, say sentences that are 12 words max, but shorter if possible. In the rest of your speech, use varied structure, rhetorical devices, flowing sentences, and short sentences. But we're talking about opening a speech right now, so ignore that. Some ways to follow my advice?

Simple words. Percussion rhythm. (Crisp, emphasized consonants). Staccato rhythm. No minimizers: no "basically," "maybe," "sort of," etc. Absolute phrases: not "this might be _____," but "this is_____." Limit tangents and parentheticals. Strong transitions. Elimination of words that don't carry information. Was reading this section easy for you? The reason is because the sentences were crisp, direct, commanding, and short. They grabbed your attention as a result.

**BAD OPENING LINES VERSUS GOOD OPENING LINES**

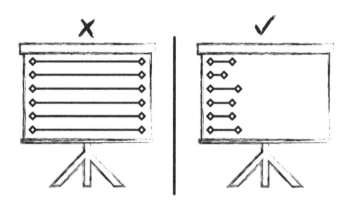

FIGURE 12: Don't overload your openings. Keep the sentences short, crisp, commanding, focused, and direct.

## ONE IDEA PER SENTENCE

One idea per sentence in your opening. Your audience is not invested to the point of caring for more than one idea per sentence. Think of it this way: the more ideas you try to add in one sentence, the less attention each of them gets. When you start a new sentence, the audience attention resets and they can devote 100% of it to the new sentence or segment. And every moment they give you their attention, it's expending (but hopefully not wasting) mental resources and calories.

So, during the opening, only convey one idea per sentence. That makes it simple. That makes it easy. Then all the sophisticated stuff can come later in your speech. Donald Trump is definitely not a *great* public speaker, but he's not *bad* either. The reason he's not bad is because he understands this rule.

Here's a sentence not following this rule: "The beloved American dream we all share is probably, in all likelihood, by my estimation just as real today, in this day and age, in the 21st century, as it was back then, when Europeans came through the gateway of opportunity that is Ellis island, usually in search of a better, more abundant life, in search of what, in this country, we call an American life, and those who say that maybe perhaps the American dream is lost, which is untrue, are the ones who, in what might be the most dire time, are essentially forgetting the basic values we stand for and have mostly stood for since the declaration of independence."

*Sigh.* This sentence has massive cognitive load, and it certainly has no place at the start of a speech (or probably anywhere else) when your audience, *ceteris paribus* (all else equal), is not convinced that they should expend the mental energy to interpret such a complex sentence. It forces your audience to store all that information in their short-term memory. And if they accidentally wipe their short-term memory because the load is too high, you lose them. The sentence suddenly makes no sense to them. This isn't ideal during your speech, but it's absolutely terrible during your opening. So, let's fix that sentence. Here it is, with all of our guidelines in play: "The American dream is real today. It is as real today as when Europeans came through Ellis island in search of a better life. They came in search of an American life. Some say that the American dream is lost. They are wrong. Those people are forgetting the basic values we stand for. They are abandoning the values we stood for since the Declaration of Independence."

Do you see what I mean? Which of those *hooks?* Which of those captivates? Which of those engages? The second speech opening does, because it is clear, it is simple, and it is fast.

If you don't follow my advice, you'll get this type of mental interaction: "Speaker: [long and complex sentence with twists, turns, parentheticals, side notes, big words, etc. right at the start of the speech] Audience's minds: [what? You think I will invest the mental energy to interpret that soup of words? Why should I?]."

Follow the advice? You get this: "Speaker: [short, crisp, and punchy sentence that is direct and easy to understand]. Audience's minds: [ah, that was easy. Low commitment. Got it.] Speaker: [another short sentence]. Audience's minds: [got it!] Speaker: [another short sentence]. Audience's minds: [I'm with you! Thanks for making this easy for me. But that last sentence intrigued me. I'm going to make more of my mental resources available for you.] Speaker: [longer sentences from this point on, if he so chooses, because he earned the right to get audience attention]."

Let me explain the truth I just illustrated: you need to use the types of sentences I described at the start of your speech because the audience hasn't afforded you the mental energy to take on difficult sentences. Every short and easy sentence the mind has to expend a small amount of resources to interpret successfully imparts meaning quickly. And, if you successfully choose the correct meaning, you earn attention. Then, you can use that attention to start with the complex sentences and more difficult and nuanced subject matter.

It is, quite frankly, entitled to start with those difficult sentences. It says "I don't have to earn your attention!" But the truth is that you do. How? By using sentences like the ones I described, and starting with a low cognitive load. Once you earn that attention, you can direct it toward complex sentences and difficult substance. (Keep in mind when speaking that sentences are indicated by fluctuations such as pauses, pitch changes, pace changes, and volume changes).

## WHAT YOUR EARLY SENTENCES SHOULD LOOK LIKE

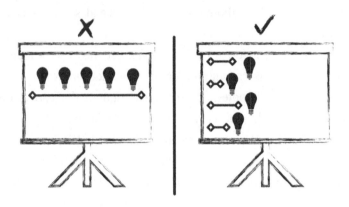

FIGURE 13: Each sentence can only hold so much weight before it overwhelms people's short-term memory banks and you lose them. There is a higher tolerance for complexity later on, but at the beginning when the information foraging dynamic is most at play, keep each sentence light, short, and focused. One idea per sentence.

## CHARTING THEIR TOLERANCE FOR COMPLEXITY

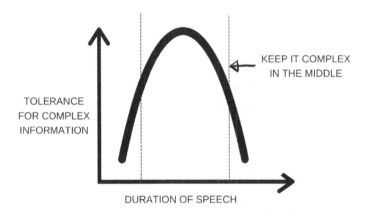

FIGURE 14: The audience has the lowest tolerance for complexity at the beginning and at the end. Keep it simple at the beginning at the end. Focus on the dynamics of attention. Present complexity in the middle.

## FAST PACE, HIGH ENERGY, INTENSITY

Want to give the strongest speech opening? Speak with fast pace. Speak with high energy. Speak with controlled intensity. Why? These all grab attention and draw people in.

## THE FIRST 15 SECONDS

Why do all of these things I told you to do? Because the first 15 seconds make or break a speech. You either win or lose based on those 15 seconds. You either grab and hold attention, or lose it. It's that simple. If you start well, you'll speak well throughout, and end well. All in all, that brings the Pareto principle back into play. Allow me to break down the Pareto principle for you in the following section.

---

**KEY INSIGHT:**

People Iteratively Reevaluate If the Object of their Focus Is the Worthiest Object to Focus On.

In the Modern Era, We Both Reevaluate And Answer In the Negative Much More Frequently.

---

## 80/20 OPENINGS

In its simplest form, the Pareto principle means that 20% of the actions produce 80% of the results. For example, in business, 20% of the customers often produce 80% of the revenue. In public speaking, your opening is much less than 20% of your speech. But it produces about 80% of the success; or rather, 100% of the subsequent success, while not produced directly by the opening, hinges upon it. The successful opening is more like a prerequisite. Now that we have discussed the foundational theories of beginning communication in such a way that you achieve magnetic presence, we will get into

**OPENINGS ARE THE PIVOT-POINT FOR MASSIVE IMPACT**

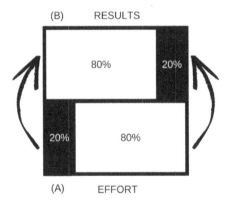

FIGURE 15: Openings (A), roughly speaking, represent 20% of the effort that creates 80% of the results (B).

## HOW TO START A SPEECH: 64 PROVEN METHODS

These 64 proven speech openings are guaranteed to start your speech off on the right foot. Why? Because they all instantly grab audience attention. They are linchpins to magnetic presence.

## QUESTION

Questions are mentally interactive. Interaction commands attention. When someone asks you a question in a one-on-one situation, you engage. It'd be rude not to. You listen, think, and respond. And when you start your speech with a question, your audience engages, listens, thinks, and mentally responds (or verbally, if you invite them to). So, start a speech with a question. It is the simplest trick in the book. "Did you know…" "How many of you have…" "Has this ever happened to you…" "Why does this happen…" "What does it lead to…" "How can we move forward…" Think of what question your audience most wants the answer to, and state the question before proceeding to answer it.

## INTERACTION

Conversations are engaging. In fact, all back-and-forth human interaction is more engaging than a one-way interaction. So, interact with your audiences if it is appropriate in the context. Call for a raise of hands. Ask for responses. Do a little back-and-forth. A little tip: when you're interacting with your audience in this way, walk forward, to be closer. That cements the "interaction paradigm." It mimics the physical closeness in which interaction usually occurs. You can even "pop-quiz" them. Ask them a bunch of questions, calling on specific people. It's so powerful. Why? Because they are thinking: "What if I get called on next? What if I'm going to miss the question? I better pay attention!" And if you have their attention in a way that is relevant to your speech, your opening is a success.

## STARTLING STATISTIC

Consider this: "A lot of people in Flint Michigan don't have clean water" versus "74% of people in Flint Michigan don't have clean water." Which is more powerful as a speech opening? The one with the startling statistic, of course. But let's take this even further. "74% of people in Flint Michigan don't have clean water. Look at your row. There are about 10 people per row. Imagine that seven of the people in your row are being poisoned by their drinking water. Imagine that the lead in the water is damaging their children's brain development. Now, of course, you might be one of the lucky three. But do you want to leave this to luck?" Attention acquired. Well done. So, the moral of this example is that you should not just throw out a startling statistic. Also connect it to the audience. Explain how that statistic would look applied to your audience. Show them why it is so shocking. Explain second and third order impacts of the statistic. Ask them to imagine the statistic applying to them.

---

**KEY INSIGHT:**

Shock Exists Where Expectations Don't. A Shocking Statistic Is So Because It Shatters Expectations.

Not All Statistics Are Equally Effective Attention-Grabbers. Not All Statistics Startle with Equally Shocking Surprise.

---

## REVEALING THE TYPE OF INFORMATION THAT CAPTIVATES

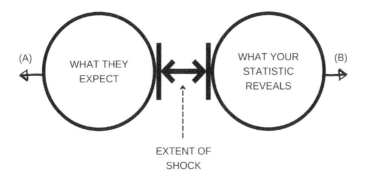

FIGURE 16: The disparity between what they expect and what your statistic reveals is the extent of the shock the statistic creates. You can make it more shocking by manipulating their expectations (A) moving further outside their base of expectations with the statistic (B), or both.

## QUOTE

This is the easiest way to start a speech. Go online. Google "quotes about [subject]." Choose one. Start with it. You have a speech opening. Make sure the quote is truly relevant. Make sure the person who said the quote is relevant. Make sure that the quote isn't too long. Make sure there's clear alignment between your subject and your quote.

## STORY

Stories have been refined over thousands of years to engage us. The basic story plot is a vehicle for information that passes stories down through the generations. Stories are extremely engaging. And what do you want for your speech opening? Engagement. So, start with a story of yours: "It all started when..." "Let me tell you a story..."

"One time, long ago, I was..." "Let me tell you a story of how this all started..." "This story will tell you everything you need to know..."

### THE FIRST TIME-TESTED STORY FRAMEWORK

FIGURE 17: A hero has a problem and meets a guide who gives him a plan to solve it and calls him to action. He acts, resulting in success or failure.

### THE SECOND TIME-TESTED STORY FRAMEWORK

FIGURE 18: A hero is called to action, succeeds temporarily, but faces failures before winning again.

## REASON

Want to know how to start a speech? A powerful way is with a reason. Start your speech opening with the reason why you are there. And align your reason with your audience's reason. Ask yourself "why am I speaking to this audience?" Ask yourself "why is this audience listening to me?" Say "I'm speaking to all of you because [insert reason that is relevant to you and your audience]."

For example: "I'm speaking to you today because there's a great threat facing our nation." "I'm speaking to you today because you are the future, and I want you to succeed." "I'm speaking to you today because if you listen closely, you'll learn exactly how to succeed in this world."

## DIRECT REQUEST

"Let me tell you..." "Listen up..." "Give me your attention, because you need to know this..." Those are all direct requests. They are powerful ways to open your speech. They are commanding. Commanding speakers get attention. Successful speech openings get attention. Why is this so effective? Because if your audience thinks "wow, this person is clearly authoritative... I'm going to let them run the show and take me along, because they clearly aren't here to waste my time," you're starting in a very strong place. An extra bonus guideline for starting your speech with a direct request is this: try to include a "because." Science shows that direct requests are more persuasive if they include a reason. And that's true even if the reason is invalid (although a valid one is obviously better). So instead of saying "let me tell you about [insert subject]," and ending it there, say "let me tell you about [insert subject], because [insert reason]."

## THE LEAD

Don't bury the lead. Don't bury your main idea and slowly build up to it. Instead, start with the lead. You don't have time to slowly and meticulously build up to your main idea. Start your speech with your main idea. There are two reasons why: you're presenting your main idea when audience attention is highest, and starting with the main idea grabs even more attention.

## SIMPLE PREMISE

Starting your speech with a simple premise means starting your speech by establishing a foundational baseline for agreement, which your audience can agree to. "I think we can all agree that this country was built on personal responsibility" is a perfect example. Why do these simple premise openings work? Because they are meaningful, but simple enough to keep cognitive load down. In other words, the simple premise is indeed a premise that lays the foundation for your speech, but it is still simple enough that your audience doesn't have to waste mental calories to understand it. It also builds immense rapport with your audience if you can start with a mutually agreeable premise.

## PVAS

PVAs are powerful visual adjectives. And when you say powerful visual adjectives, your audience can't help but imagine them in their mind's eye. This is a proven way to open your speech with impact. If you say "sunset" to someone, they can't help but see a sunset in their minds. But "sunset" isn't a PVA. It isn't even an adjective. PVAs must be adjectives that are specific (a distinct aspect of the noun you're attaching them to), detail oriented (focused on the small details of the noun), and concrete (something physically visible). "Striking" is not concrete. "Orange" is. Further, they must be evocative (focused on evoking a visceral emotional reaction) and open (not so specific that the audience can't "fill in the blanks" to their individual desire). Here are some PVAs that you can apply to "sunset," that fulfill those requirements: "orange" "bright" "shimmering." Here are some PVAs that are not powerful. They are just "visual adjectives," and don't work the same way: "colorful" "beautiful" "striking." These are not specific, concrete, or detail-oriented. "Orange, bright, shimmering sunset" paints a distinct mental image. "Colorful, beautiful, striking sunset" does not.

---

**KEY INSIGHT:**

# Powerful Visual Adjectives And Compelling Verbs Project Images in the Theater of Imagination.

# Using Sound to Create Sight In the Mind's Eye Is a Deeply Influential and Moving Power.

---

## VAKOG SENSES

These are so powerful. If you liked PVAs, you're going to love the VAKOG senses. What are the VAKOG senses? V: visual. A: auditory. K: kinesthetic (feeling). O: olfactory. G: gustatory. Here's the process:

Decide on a clear visualization of a desired future outcome. Paint a mental movie in your audience's mind of this future. Use each of the VAKOG senses to paint this mental movie. (Or conversely, you can paint a vivid movie of a negative future outcome, or both a positive and negative future outcome to build immense persuasive contrast and captivate attention). Like PVAs, when you use the VAKOG senses to paint a mental movie, your audience can't help getting entrapped in it. Let's say you're selling a business solution. Let's say it's time to open your speech. Which of these two sentences paints a clearer image? Non-VAKOG: "You'll be more successful." VAKOG: "You'll *see* 20% more money when you open your financial statements; you'll *hear* constant praise from your associates; you'll *feel* relaxed every day at work; you'll *taste* the bitter adrenaline of excitement and fast progress instead of being disengaged."

## CONCRETE IMAGE

Here's the step-by-step method: Visualize the audience outcome yourself. Describe the outcome in one sentence. Write it down. Answer this question: "if I were to make a movie of this sentence, what would I point the camera at?" Engineer this "concrete," or physical, tangible image of a positive outcome into your speech opening. In other words: tie abstract concepts, like "be more successful," to concrete, physical, tangible changes in the real world.

## IMAGINE

A bullet–proof way to start a speech is to ask your audience to imagine something. "Imagine that you had to sacrifice your values one by one to make ends meet. That's what's happening to the people of the United States." "Imagine that every gulp of water your children drank was slowly poisoning their minds. That's the reality of people living in Flint Michigan." "Imagine that you hear of the most evil, heinous, and inhumane crime possible. I'll spare you the details. Imagine that you can't tell the police, because you'll be separated from your family and deported. That's the reality for undocumented immigrants across the country." That's some powerful stuff. It will instantly captivate your audience. It is an excellent way to start a speech.

## SHOCK

Start with a shocking statement. Shock captures attention. Attention is the prerequisite of a good speech opening. Shocking statements are those that cause indignation, cause offense, cause surprise, cause dismay, and cause negative emotions. Now, you're probably wondering, "so I'm supposed to offend my audience?" No. But what if you told them about someone who said something that offends them? For example: "The Republican nominee thinks this district is filled with people who have no personal responsibility, who aren't willing to pull themselves up by the bootstraps, and who are not hard working. But I know that's not who you are. These circumstances aren't your fault." Or, as a counter-example: "The Democratic nominee thinks that you need government handouts to take care of yourselves. I say no: big government should get out of your way, and treat you like the self-sufficient people you are." You see how they are shocking their audiences by offending them without being the person who's doing the offending?

## DIRECTLY RELEVANT

Start your speech with a statement that is directly relevant to your audience. "You are all going to suffer in the next ten years because of climate change." "Your town, this town, where we are right now, is at risk of completely flooding due to rising sea levels." "You are projected to pay an extra 30% in state taxes to make up for climate change related preparations."

Here's what your audience (indeed, most people) are thinking 24/7/365: "Me, me, me!' So how should you start a speech? In a way that addresses this. In other words, like this: "You, you, you!"

### "WIIFM?"

"WIIFM?" stands for "What's in it for me?" That's what your audience is thinking, and that's the question you should answer with your speech opening. Tell your audience these what they gain from listening, how your speech benefits them, and why your speech will help them. Do so subtly and tactfully.

### PROMISE

Start your speech with a promise. This builds immense trust, and instantly grabs attention. "I promise that I'll teach you exactly how to [insert action]." "I promise that you'll learn exactly why [insert reason]." "I promise that you'll walk away with [insert outcome]."

### PREVIEW

A powerful speech opening is a preview. For example: "We're going to be talking about the threats to our nation, and how to solve them." "Today, you're going to learn the basics of financial planning and then three simple action steps to get started." "I'm going to tell you why this party – your party, our party – can save America." Why is this effective? Because it builds massive intrigue, curiosity, and anticipation for what you're going to say. A "preview" opening is essentially telling your audience what you're going to tell them. And you can even attach a time limit to it. For example: "I'm going to prove to you that [insert claim], in the next ten minutes."

## YES-LADDER

Yes-ladders draw people in like a mental vortex. I especially love using them in speech openings. Why? Because they create interaction, grab attention, and build rapport. All you have to do is ask a series of questions to which your audience will think "yes." Doing so builds immense trust. The obvious "yes" questions start, and then you build up to more controversial, provocative questions. "Do you think America could be better? [Yes! I do.] At the end of every month, do you wish you had more money? [Obviously!] Do you wish you paid less taxes? Would that help? [Well, that would make things easier for my family.] Do you feel like you're paying excessive taxes that are being wasted? [Maybe. I don't know. That could be the case. It certainly feels excessive.]" And you don't have to present this opening through questions: conditionals work as well. "If you believe (insert easy 'yes'), if you believe (insert bigger 'yes'), if you believe (insert bigger 'yes')... then..." After thinking "yes" four or five times, your audience will be fully on board with you.

**VISUALIZING THE PRINCIPLE OF PERSUASIVE MOMENTUM**

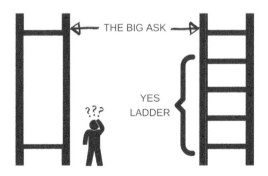

FIGURE 19: If you begin with the big ask, you are not giving people any persuasive rungs they can climb to reach the

big ask. If you instead begin with a "yes ladder," you are giving people the opportunity to climb the ladder to reach the big ask. This increases agreement.

## POSITIVE CONSPIRACY

Conspiracies captivate attention. And starting your speech with one is a proven way to grab attention from the start. Also, a good conspiracy is the basis of a solid friendship and bond between people. Why? You *trust* your co-conspirators; else the conspiracy fails. (I'm guessing here. I've never been in a major conspiracy. Except for – you know what? Never mind. Let's move on.)

For example: "I'm going to let you in on a little-known secret." This method also builds trust. This is a "positive conspiracy," in which you and your audience members are the co-conspirators.

## NEGATIVE CONSPIRACY

This is a proven speech opening. In fact, it's been used in the world's great speeches by the world's great speakers. What's the difference between a positive conspiracy and a negative conspiracy? In a positive conspiracy, you are entering into a conspiracy with your audience. In a negative conspiracy, you are unveiling a conspiracy against you and your audience. And when you start a speech with that, you instantly grab attention. But there are some important guidelines: don't say the word "conspiracy," unless it really is a full-blown conspiracy. The word conspiracy is associated with outlandish YouTube videos. Instead, say words like "secret plot," "hidden, little-known ploy," "underground attack," etc. These phrases have the same impact minus the appearance of craziness. An example of a brilliant negative conspiracy opening: "The high office of President has been used to foment a plot to destroy the American's freedom, and before I leave office I must inform the citizen of his plight." – John F. Kennedy at

Columbia University. If it's good enough for JFK, it's good enough for you and me.

## COGNITIVE DISSONANCE

Make people see a conflict between any of the following: Who they think they are and reality. Their beliefs and reality. What they want to have and reality. This guarantees that they feel a strong urge to close that gap. They feel strong dissonance. They feel anxiety. And if you can make your audience feel this cognitive dissonance, you have their attention. This is a great way to start a speech.

**HOW CREATING COGNITIVE PAIN CAN WORK IN YOUR FAVOR**

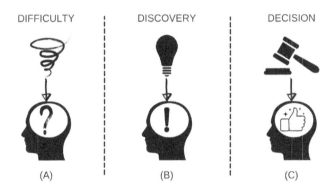

DIFFICULTY      DISCOVERY      DECISION

(A)      (B)      (C)

FIGURE 20: Present cognitive and problem-solving difficulty that creates uncertainty and cognitive dissonance (A). Then, present a discovery that resolves the cognitive dilemma and eases the pain, creating certainty (B). Then, inspire a decision to adopt the discover (C).

## INOCULATION

To quote from one of my favorite books, *Cashvertising*: "The Inoculation Theory is used to reinforce a consumer's existing attitudes toward a product or service by presenting a 'weak' argument that tricks the consumer into defending his position and therefore strengthening his attitude. The three steps are: Warn of an impending attack; Make a weak attack; and Encourage a strong defense. Consumer psychologists warn that your attack must be weak. Otherwise, you risk having the opposite effect and weakening or changing your prospects' attitudes." For example: "The Republican nominee will attack our platform. *(Warn of impending attack)*. They will say we want to spend frivolously. *(Weak attack)*. But is it frivolous spending to help single mothers give their children an education? Is it frivolous spending to make sure homeless people aren't dying on the streets? Is it frivolous spending to give healthcare to people who would die without it? Is it frivolous to spend money to save life? *(Strong defense)*."

---

**KEY INSIGHT:**

The Line Between Rhetoric And Advertising, Marketing, and Consumer Psychology Is a Fine One, And In Some Places So Faint It Is Practically Invisible.

Make Of This What You Will.

---

## SECRET

People love secrets. This opening will create mystery, build suspense, and grab attention. All you have to do is tease a secret, and use secrecy phrases. For example, words like: "Hidden" "Little–known" "Secret" "Obscure" "Unknown" "Veiled" etc. "Today, I'm going to let you all in on a little-known, hidden, insider secret. That's right. This obscure fact of finance is closely-guarded and veiled by the top financial firms in the country. But today, I'm going to lift that veil."

## EASE

If you can promise a quick and easy method to solve a problem or achieve an outcome, then you have a powerful speech opening. People love ease. People love simplicity. People love guidance, and straight-forward step-by-step directions. People are lazy. And if you satisfy their laziness, you will start a speech with influence. For example: "I'm going to teach you an easy, three-step process to immediately make more sales with little effort." "You're going to love this easy, simple, step-by-step process to audit your finances." "This process makes [insert goal] possible without [insert difficulty usually attached to goal]."

## NEW DISCOVERY

Novelty hooks audiences. New information is captivating. Humans love novelty. News is always new. We crave it. So, start your speech by offering news to your audience. "Something unbelievable just happened, and I'm going to tell you right now." "You won't believe what just happened..." "Something new is on the horizon..."

## BENEFIT STATEMENTS

It's a simple but powerful way to start a speech. I like to break it down to a simple four-step process: Figure out what your audience wants. Promise to give that to them in your opening. Repeatedly touch on that audience desire. Use the word "you" in a sentence with the audience desire. If your audience is a bunch of salesmen and saleswomen, start your speech like this: "I am going to teach *you* exactly how to make more sales." Financiers? "I am going to teach *you* exactly how to survive the next recession." People concerned about new legislation? "I am going to tell *you* exactly why the new bill is nothing to worry about."

## MENTAL MOVIE

Paint a mental movie. People will imagine what you tell them to imagine. So, if you want to start your speech by illustrating a scene, paint a mental movie. Use PVAs, the VAKOG senses, and storytelling. Tell a concrete, highly specific story using the VAKOG senses and visually stimulating scenes that evoke emotional responses with PVAs.

## RADICAL TRUTH-TELLING

Let's say there's an elephant in the room. Your audience knows it, you know it, but nobody is talking about it. Maybe you wonder if it's a good idea to bring it up or not. Do it. Why? Because it's radical truth-telling, it builds immense trust and respect, and also functions as an effective speech opening. For example: "Alright, the obvious truth nobody else wants to talk about is..." "Let's be honest about the truth that..." "What's really going on here, and what nobody else seems willing to point out, is that..."

## THIS IS THE SINGLE BIGGEST COMMUNICATION MISTAKE

FIGURE 21: If there is a big elephant in the room, don't skirt around it. Take it head on. Slay the dragon.

## RAPPORT-INVITATION

We talked about interaction, remember? It's attention–grabbing, captivating, and builds the speaker to audience connection. So, let's talk about the rapport-invitation. These speech openings start your speech in a way that makes your audience feel like they are being invited into an engaging conversation, a friend wants to talk to them about something interesting, and your speech is not going to be a passive listening experience for them. For example: "I want to have a conversation with you all about…" "Let's talk about…" "I think it's time for a conversation about…" These are especially useful for more casual speeches designed to draw people into a conversational relationship with the speaker.

## TRIAD OPENING

This one is so cool. Why? Because it immediately constructs the public speaking triad: the three-way connection between speaker, audience, and idea. They must all be connected to each other. So, all you have to do for this opening is connect your audience to yourself, connect your audience to your idea, and connect your idea to yourself. How? Here's an example. Audience to self connection: "This was actually my alma mater. I used to sit in that seat every time guest speakers would visit." Audience to idea connection: "You might be wondering what this bill has to do with you. It has everything to do with you. If this legislation is passed, you will all pay higher taxes and receive lower benefits. Your lives will simply be less abundant." Idea to self connection: "I spent almost a decade as a tax analyst at the Brookings institute, and I know a bad bill when I see it."

### BEGIN AT THE BEGINNING (OF COMMUNICATION THEORY)

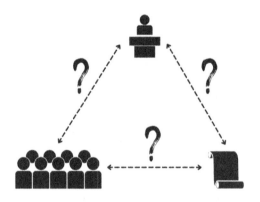

FIGURE 22: Begin by forming a three-way connection between the speaker, the audience, and the subject.

### HERE AND NOW

This opening centers audience attention in the present moment. And this means they'll probably give it to you, if your communication is clearly the most interesting thing happening in the present moment. How do you use this opening? By relating something you're saying back to the current time and the current moment. For example: "As we speak right now in this room, across the world [insert what's happening across the world]." "In this exact moment, while I'm talking to you in this auditorium, [insert what's happening]." "Every second that goes by right now (snap fingers three times) the Government spends $1,000 dollars (snap fingers three times). Every time I snap, that's another $1,000 gone."

## PERSUASION WORDS

Wondering how to start a speech? Use the words: "you," "new," "because," "instantly," "easy," "results," "proven," "free." Why? Because these are the eight most persuasive words in the English language. For example: "Now you can instantly get easy results with this new but proven method, and because it's free, you can try it as soon as this speech is over. Let's get right into it..."

## SHOW OF HANDS

Ask your audience for a show of hands. Poll them. "How many of you have heard of [insert subject]?" "How many of you believe [insert viewpoint]? "How many of you believe [insert viewpoint]?" "How many of you are aware that [insert fact]?" This physical interaction through a show of hands instantly engages them.

## CONVERSATION

If you really want to go all in on interaction, which builds more attention, engagement, and interest, then enter a conversation with your audience. Ask them where they are from. Ask them for their thoughts. Ask them any question related to your subject. Pop-quiz them. Then, when someone responds, build a brief conversation with that audience member, before repeating that whole process a few times. Nice, easy, friendly, inviting, and effective, although not appropriate in every single setting (none of these openings are).

## CONTRARIAN APPROACH

This speech opening is one of my personal favorites. Here's the step-by-step process: Find a common incorrect belief related to your subject. Start your speech by debunking that myth. For example: "Trickle-down economics doesn't actually exist. It has never once been proposed by a single Republican in the history of the country."

## SOUNDBITE

What's a soundbite? The dictionary says: "A short extract from a recorded interview, chosen for its pungency or appropriateness." Politicians everywhere are striving to get some juicy soundbites. But most of them fail. A successful soundbite must be meaningful, substantive, and relevant. It must also have rhythm, cadence, and strong verbal delivery. Most successful soundbites are also combative. They usually also evoke a common but complex feeling and summarize it in one simple sentence. Starting your speech with a soundbite guarantees respect and attention.

## WHAT IF

Start your speech with a "what-if" scenario. These invite your audience into a scenario. They are prompted to think and consider the question. They ask themselves, "how would I react in this situation?" Some examples: "What if you knew that a slow, steady threat was going to attack you? That's what's happening to the United States." "What if you couldn't drink tap water? What if your tap water poisoned you? What if you drank it before knowing what would happen? That's the unfortunate reality for people in Flint Michigan." "What if you could guarantee financial security for the rest of your life? What if you could make a decision today that would guarantee financial freedom? What if you didn't have to do anything, but could trust an expert to take care of it all? That's the reality for clients of this firm." You can also string together multiple "what-if" sentences, as you can see from the examples.

## HISTORICAL REFERENCE

You might not believe what I'm about to say: starting your speech with a historical reference is actually *not* a sure-fire way to bore your audiences to death. In fact, it's an easy and effective way to start your speech. Starting a speech with a historical reference is effective if you follow this formula: Find a historical reference similar to your subject. Find the analogous similarities between the reference and your subject. Prompt your audience to look for similarities between what's happening now and what happened in your reference. Present the reference. Present the similarities to the present. Why does this work? People love history. Not necessarily as an academic discipline, but as the subject of a story. So, if you can "story-tell" the historical reference, you get their attention. But more importantly, people understand that the best lens through which to view the present is often the past. So, when you start your speech with a historical reference.

## CALL THEM OUT

This one is high-risk. Call out their deficiencies. "I'll be brutally honest with you. You're full of excuses. Maybe you say..." "Let me tell you the truth about yourselves. You've probably thought to yourself 'well, times are tight right now, I don't think it's safe to invest.' Or 'this bonus check isn't enough to invest, but it's good for a vacation!' Or even 'let me just save it, to be safe.' These are all useless excuses holding you back from financial freedom. And if none of those excuses sound like you, then I promise you that you have your own set." When you call them out in a respectful (but assertive) way, and in a way that is at least slightly accurate, you get instant attention and respect.

## CHALLENGE

Start your speech with a challenge. "I challenge you to invest 20% of your income. I bet you won't be able to do it. You'll come up with a host of excuses. But hey, maybe I'm wrong. It's up to you to prove me wrong." Instant attention. Instant respect. Instant interest. And as a bonus, you might even get your audience to take your challenge, but only if the rest of your speech is as effective as this opening.

**KEY INSIGHT:**

# One Of the Best Persuasive Angles Borders on Inspiration: Challenge People to Be the Best They Could Be.

# Challenge Them to Fulfill Their Potential, Take Personal Responsibility, Act with Virtue, And Face their Fears.

## DIRECTION

A challenge is commanding. A direction is even more commanding. So, start your speech by giving your audience a direction. "I want you to save 20% of your income from now on, and you will see not only how easy it really is but the peace of mind it gives you." "You are all going to save 20% of your income after I show you exactly how to budget effectively." "This is what I want you to do: save 20% of your income, and pay 10% less taxes with these hidden deductions. I'll show you how."

## SET EXPECTATIONS

Start your speech by setting the expectations for the talk. "By the end of this speech, you're going to know exactly how to excel at financial planning." "I'm going to show you exactly how to simplify your lives and find inner peace." "By the end of this talk, you should expect to become informed investors who are capable of managing their money." Benefit-driven expectations make your audience anticipate the rest of your speech. You excite them for the rest of your speech. You make them see you as the source of value. You make them trust you.

## SILENCE

Start your speech with silence. Instead of getting on your stage, jumping straight into it, and looking hurried and frazzled, do this: slowly walk to your speaking position. Look at the audience. Look around. Make eye contact. Smile. Wait 10 seconds. 15. Be silent. Be still. Then, begin. It has a... *strange* effect on your audience. It's indescribable. And it's even more impressive if they are all speaking loudly amongst themselves while waiting for you, and you don't silence them with your words, but with your silence. That said, don't take this too far. If silence doesn't work, have a backup opening.

## UNDERSTANDING THE PRINCIPLE OF ATTENTION-GRABBING

SET OF POSSIBLE OCCURRENCES

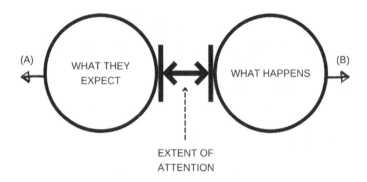

FIGURE 23: The disparity between what they expect and what happens is the extent of the attention you receive. Change what they expect (A), what happens (B), or both.

## THE LITTLE-KNOWN SECRET OF CONFIDENCE

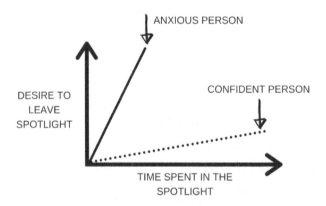

FIGURE 24: An anxious person in the spotlight wants to leave the spotlight much more quickly than a confident person. They would never stand in silence, extending the time spent in the spotlight. They rush and stumble. A confident person, on the other hand, is willing to spend much more time in the spotlight. Full confidence is occupying the spotlight for however long is necessary.

## COMPLIMENT

Start your speech by complimenting your audience. Want to know a secret of effective compliments? Here's the secret: tell them they excel at the exact thing they are insecure about. Tell them they are the person they want to be. Tell them they have what they have been chasing. This requires three things: perception, people-reading skills, and prior knowledge of your audience.

## HOPE

Start your speech by giving your audience hope. "You may have heard about the threat facing our nation. But today I want to make the case for hope." "You all know how difficult it is to plan your financial future. But I promise you that it will be better. I'll show you how." "We are at a crossroads right now. We can give up, or we can embrace hope and keep going. Which will it be?" Hope is a gift. Give it to the audience, and they'll give you attention and respect.

**HOPE LIGHTENS AN UNBEARABLE BURDEN**

FIGURE 25: A hardship plus hope in the face of struggle is a significantly lighter burden than only hardship.

**GIVE THEM THE GREATEST GIFT TO EARN ATTENTION**

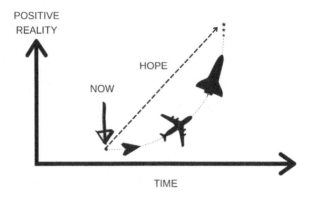

FIGURE 26: Hope is looking onward to a vision of a better reality, and doing so with faith in its realization.

## DISCUSSION

Now, this isn't always a good way to start your talk. Use this when your audience is small – less than 40 people – your audience members know each other, and your speech would benefit from something like this. To do it, all you have to do is tell your audience members to talk to one another for a little. For example: "Before I get into it, I want you all to talk amongst yourselves. Discuss why you think we are facing this problem." Make sure the prompt is specific. Then, you can even call on people and ask them what conclusion they've reached with each other. Simple, but effective.

## VISUAL

Start your speech by directing people's attention to a visual. People love visuals. We process visual information much faster than non-visual information. And directing your audience's attention cements your control of it. Every time you say "turn your attention to this visual," or "I want you to imagine," or any statement directing audience attention, what you're doing is cementing your control of their attention. A visual can be graphic data, graphs, charts (as long as they are not too complex), an evocative image of the subject, or a picture from your life that's related to the subject. For example, someone speaking about the water crisis in Flint Michigan could project a picture of the muddy water.

## PURPOSE

Tell your audience the purpose of the speech. "I'm here to liberate you from financial stress." "I'm here to tell you why you should vote for a Democrat." "I'm here to guide you towards inner peace and simplicity." Want to open your speech properly? Weave audience benefits into your opening. This not just for purpose openings, but for all openings you'll learn. For example, let's revisit the previous three: "I'm here to liberate you from financial stress" – the benefit is liberation from stress. "I'm here to tell you why you should vote for a Democrat" – the benefit is political understanding and clarity. "I'm here to guide you towards inner peace and simplicity" – the benefit is inner peace and simplicity.

## JOKE

Start a speech with a joke. I'll be honest: being funny isn't my specialty. If I am a good public speaker, it is not because of my humor. I am only ever funny by accident. So, I refuse to leave you with useless, boilerplate advice on how to write a good joke. If you're funny? You'll know how. If not? Don't use this opening.

## GENERIC YOU STATEMENT

People love themselves. We talked about that. They love hearing about themselves, thinking about themselves, and being spoken to about themselves. So, start your speech with a "you statement."

What's a "you statement?" It's just a statement about your audience. It doesn't necessarily have to include a benefit. For example: "You are making avoidable financial mistakes." "You are being cheated by your current political party." "You are able to achieve amazing things under the right circumstances." Get it? Easy, but elegant, and definitely still powerful if they don't include benefits.

## SURVIVE-AND-THRIVE

People only listen to you if you communicate about something that helps them survive and thrive. I learned this wisdom from Donald Miller of Storybrand, author of *Building a Storybrand.* Human beings are wired to direct attention toward information that can confer some adaptive advantage, helping them survive and propagate. Opening a speech in this manner is simple: consider the most impactful second and third order stakes of your subject (if not the immediate ones), and extract the aspect of your subject that directly ties to the well-being of the audience.

### HOW TO PERSUADE BY APPEALING TO GENETIC EVOLUTION

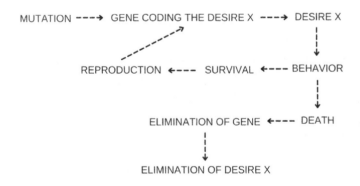

FIGURE 27: A genetic mutation coded a desire, leading an organism to have that desire. This desire created behavior

that resulted in survival, reproduction, and the spread of the mutation and desire, or death, and the elimination of the gene creating the desire as well as the desire itself.

## WHAT'S AT STAKE?

People only care about your message if you tell them why it matters. In other word, your audience must understand the stakes of what you're saying. So that's exactly how to start a speech with impact. Tell your audience the stakes of your subject. For example: "The future of our nation is at stake." "Your ability to survive the coming recession is at stake." "The lives of thousands of children in Michigan are at stake."

### HOW TO ENGAGE WITH INFLUENCE AND IMPACT

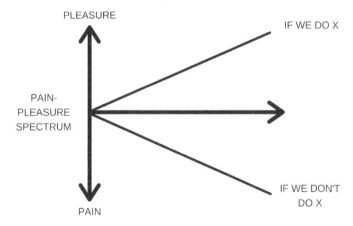

FIGURE 28: Present a crossroads between massive success and massive failure; between great pleasure and great pain. This captivates attention like nothing else.

## FEAR

Fear demands attention. So, start your speech by stirring fear. Fear is the single most motivational emotion. People take a vast number of actions simply because fear tells them to. Some examples of how to use fear: "Listen. Millions of criminals are pouring across our borders." "This president is literally an existential threat to our country." "Climate change will flood this town. Can you afford to buy a new house?"

## STRAIGHT-TO-BUSINESS

Maybe you don't have much time. Maybe your audience is in a rush. Maybe you know your audience would appreciate brevity. If these apply, start your speech with a "straight-to-business" opening. For example: "Listen up. I know you all are busy, so I'll get right into it." "I'm going to save your time and jump right into it." "Instead of wasting your precious time, I'll tell you exactly what you need to know." These all instantly grab attention. Why? Because they are all no-nonsense, time-saving openings.

---

**KEY INSIGHT:**

The Straight-to-Business Style Carries a Subtle Implication of Rhetoric-Free Communication.

This Subtle Implication of Rhetoric-Free Communication Is A Perfect Example of Rhetoric.

---

## EXCHANGE

These are commanding and instantly get you respect from your audience. Tell them what you're going to give them and your "asking price." Here's how: "Give me ten minutes and I'll teach you the secrets of financial freedom." "Give me your attention and I'll give you everything you need to know about investing." "If you give me five minutes of your time, I'll show you how to save 20% on taxes with hidden deductions." If you're offering way more value than the time and attention you're asking for, then you're guaranteed to get the audience's attention. This is always true, but this speech opening makes it clear and explicit. And if you're providing less value than the time and attention you're asking for, that's a bigger problem.

## PROVOCATIVE STATEMENT

Provocation grabs attention. So, start your speech with a provocative statement. Provocative statements are those that go against common consensus, mildly offend people, and are regarded as taboo. If you have what it takes, consider starting your speech with a provocative statement. And it's a delicate balance you must strike between excessive provocation and an appropriate amount of it: the kind of provocation that gives you an edge versus the kind of provocation that puts people on edge to the point of discomfort.

## PROBLEM-SOLUTION

Start your speech with a mini problem-solution structure. When you are speaking to people, persuading, or even informing, you are trying to get them to adopt a solution to a problem. But does your solution make any sense if you don't talk about the problem? No. People will pay you attention if you talk about the problem they have that you are solving. "You came here because you have a problem. Your finances are not in order. Your finances may not survive the recession. Your finances are most definitely not as well-organized and protected as they could be. And the solution is a simple process which I'll teach you in this brief presentation. Problems grab attention. Solutions grab attention. Problems plus solutions are fundamental.

## THE PERSUASIVE MAGIC OF THE PASA STRUCTURE

| STRUCTURE | "PASA" Structure | | | |
|---|---|---|---|---|
| BEHAVIORAL DUALITY | Escape | | Approach | |
| SEMANTIC DUALITY | Problem | | Solution | |
| EMOTIONAL DUALITY | Pain | | Pleasure | |
| TEMPORAL DUALITY | Now | | Later | |
| EXISTENTIAL DUALITY | Here | | There | |
| DESIRE DUALITY | Aversion | | Desire | |
| MODAL DUALITY | Chaos | | Order | |
| STATE DUALITY | Actual | | Potential | |
| KAIROS DUALITY | Conflict | | Resolution | |
| THE SEQUENCE | **Problem** | **Agitate** | **Solution** | **Agitate** |

## DON'T OFFER ME A LIFE-RAFT ON LAND

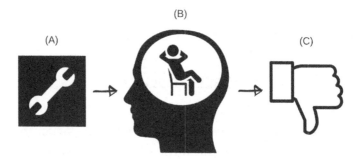

FIGURE 29: If you offer me a solution (A) when the world is telling me to relax (B), I will reject it (C).

**I'LL GIVE YOU $1,000,000 FOR THE RAFT**

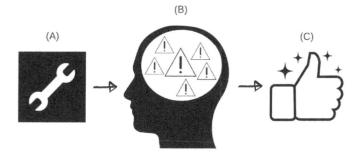

FIGURE 30: If you offer me a solution (A) when the world is yelling at me "PROBLEM, FIX IT, EMERGENCY, PROBLEM, DO SOMETHING, DANGER, FIX IT< URGENT, CODE RED, URGENT, CODE RED, URGENT, CODE RED," (B), I will do anything for it (C). The desire for a solution is directly proportional to the scope of the problem it solves; to the scope of the pain the problem causes and its urgency.

## LOSS

People fear loss. If you tell them they are set up to lose something, they will listen. But before I tell you how, remember that people fear losing something they have more than they seek gaining something new. It's called loss aversion. So how do you use loss aversion? Here's how: "Republicans want to take away your healthcare." Or, "Democrats want to tell you that you can't go to your doctor." People will instantly pay attention if you warn them of an incoming loss. It's how we're wired.

## TAKE ADVANTAGE OF THE LOSS AVERSION PRINCIPLE

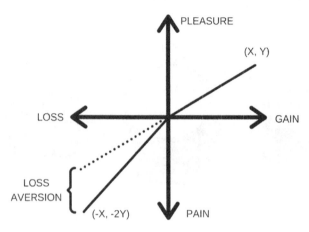

FIGURE 31: Humans feel the pain of loss more than the pleasure of gain. Some people feel up to twice as much pain from a loss as they do pleasure from an equivalent gain. This is known as loss aversion.

## WHY-RESPONSES

The inner machinations of this brilliant speech opening are complicated. It has to do with "purpose-convergence" and behavioral theory. But executing this speech opening is easy. All you have to do is follow this simple three-step process: Ask your audience why they are attending your presentation (if it makes sense in the context), or what they want to gain from it. Repeat this question for a few audience members, or ask for a raise of hands if a previous reason applies. Tell them that you are also there for the same reasons.

For example: "I want to ask you all, why are you here? What motivated you to attend this event? Just raise your hands and share your answer out loud. The gentleman in the front row, with the green tie. [Answer: I wanted to learn how to take control of my finances]. Excellent. How about the lady in the second row with the blue coat? [Answer: I just got a nice bonus and I want to learn how to invest it]. Who else shares these feelings? Raise your hand if you can relate to wanting to learn how to take control of your finances and invest surplus income. [Answer: 70% of the audience raises their hands]. That's great. Because I'm here to teach you exactly how to take control of your finances once and for all, and a huge part of that is learning how to invest extra income when you have it." Easy to execute. Here's why this is so powerful as a speech opening: you're essentially telling your audiences that "I'm here to give you exactly what you came here to get."

## STARTLING ADMISSION

Start your speech with a startling admission. It's an insanely powerful way to grab attention, create a speaker to audience bond, and gain trust through vulnerability. For example: "A long time ago, I struggled with my finances. At the end of every month, sitting at the kitchen table trying to make ends meet was something I always dreaded. Honestly. It was such a difficult time in my life." "Yes, I'm running to be the Republican nominee. But I used to be a silent Democrat." Presenting these statements shows your humanity. It makes you connect on a personal, human level with your audience. And through this deep, meaningful bond forged by making a vulnerable admission, you start your speech with impact and attention.

**Email Peter D. Andrei, the author of the Speak for Success collection and the President of Speak Truth Well LLC directly.**

**pandreibusiness@gmail.com**

**INTRIGUE LIES IN BREAKING EXPECTATION**

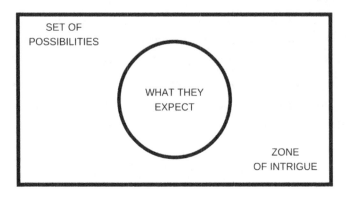

FIGURE 32: The zone of intrigue exists wherever their expectations don't. You can further subdivide this into more useful categories: "appropriate unexpected possibilities, useful unexpected possibilities, inappropriate unexpected possibilities," etc.

## I WAS THERE

Start your speech with this simple, two-step process: figure out the struggles your audience is dealing with, and tell them how you were going through them in the past. For example, let's say the audience is struggling with a lack of financial knowledge. An expert financial planner giving an educational presentation can say "I struggled for a long time because of my lack of financial knowledge," and break down the specifics and emotionally evocative circumstances of his difficult past. This creates immense relatability. Relatability produces an audience to speaker connection. And this, in turn, leads to attention.

## PLAY ON A SAYING

Take a saying, a parable, or a piece of long-lasting wisdom, and alter it in a way that it is recognizable but different, or apply it in a new way. For example: "Donald Trump once said 'divide and conquer.' Just kidding. That was Sun Tzu in *The Art of War*, about 2,000 years ago. But that very same principle is working for President Trump today, and locking the Democratic party out of legislating."

## GUIDE

Start your speech by presenting yourself as a guide. A guide must have authority and empathy. For example: "I feel your pain; I felt it myself. I was in the same place. And I know how to fix it. I know how to move forward."

### REVERSE-ENGINEER THE CRITICAL STORY COMPONENT

FIGURE 33: Perceiving a guide in and of itself is attention-grabbing. We are hyper-responsive to guides. Guides are tremendously useful. Guides help us survive and thrive. You can cut out the guide step of the story framework and use it on its own. The two key components of a guide are empathy and authority.

## SPEECH OPENING FORMULAS TO INSTANTLY CAPTIVATE

These following speech openings are proven, step-by-step formulas: simple molds you can fill in with your specific words. Keep in mind that they are generalized examples, and many of the words are figurative and can be shifted around to make more sense in the specific context of your message as long as you maintain the general tenor of the formula and the steps in their proper sequence. And while some of the examples use "we" while others use "you," it is possible to retool all of the formulas to speak either about what "we need to do" or what "you need to do." I recommend "we," as it is an inclusive pronoun that puts you and your audience on the same team and the same page.

---

**KEY INSIGHT:**

Rhetorical Formulas Offer Guardrails Designed to Keep You On a Path Your Audience Is Interested In Following. And Nothing About Them Sounds or Appears Formulaic. Done Well, They Sound Spontaneous.

---

## AGREE, PROMISE, PREVIEW

Agree: "I know exactly what it feels like to [insert pain point]. I know how difficult it can be. I agree that it needs to change." Promise: "And I promise that it doesn't have to be this way." Preview: "With this [insert what you are offering], you can [insert benefit] and escape [insert pain point].

### MASTER BOTH CONSCIOUS AND SUBCONSCIOUS INFLUENCE

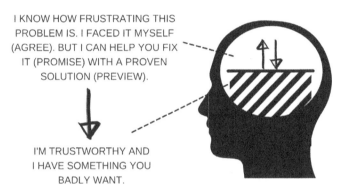

FIGURE 34: The APP framework presents unspoken words in subtext, sending them directly to the subconscious mind. Many of these frameworks do too.

## PROMISE, PREVIEW, PROMISE

Promise: "I promise that by the end of this speech, you'll [insert benefit]." Preview: "You'll learn the hidden secrets of [insert subject], like [insert tease]." Promise: "And I promise that these hidden secrets will help you [insert benefit]."

## OUTCOME, PROMISE, PREVIEW

Outcome: "By the end of this speech, you'll [insert positive outcome]." Promise: "I promise that you'll achieve [insert outcome] with an easy, simple, step-by-step process proven to work time and time again." Preview: "For example, many people report this process only taking ten minutes."

## OUTCOME, OUTCOME, OUTCOME, PROMISE, PROOF, PREVIEW

Outcome: "By the end of this speech, you'll [insert positive outcome]." Outcome: "You'll also be able to [insert second positive outcome]." Outcome: "And, even better, you'll learn exactly how to [insert third positive outcome]." Promise: "I promise that you can achieve these with ease, if you pay attention." Proof: "I recently contacted ten people from my last presentation. Seven of them said they achieved [insert outcome one], [insert outcome two], and [insert outcome three]." Preview: "And the best part is that they did it exactly like I told them to, with [insert brief preview]."

## PROBLEM, AGITATE, SOLUTION

Problem: "We are all struggling with [insert problem], and the consequence of that problem, [insert consequence]." Agitate: "If we don't solve [insert problem] soon, we will face [insert bigger, emotionally stimulating consequence]." Solution: "But have an idea as to how we can solve [insert problem] and how to prevent [insert consequence one] and [insert consequence two]."

## PROBLEM, AGITATE, AGITATE, AGITATE, SOLUTION

Problem: "We are all struggling with [insert problem], and the consequence of that problem, [insert consequence]." Agitate: "If we don't solve [insert problem] soon, we will face [insert bigger consequence]." Agitate: "This will lead to [insert bigger problem], and [insert bigger problem again]." Agitate: "By the end of it all, we will experience [insert emotional consequences]." Solution: "But I know how we can solve [insert problem] and how to avoid these crippling consequences."

## BENEFIT, BENEFIT, BENEFIT, DELAY

Benefit: "Today, I'll teach you how to [insert benefit]." Benefit: "You'll be able to achieve [insert benefit two]." Benefit: "And you'll even learn how to [insert benefit three]." Delay: "I'll teach you all this in a few minutes. But first…"

## QUESTION, PROMISE, PREVIEW

Question: "Are you aware that [insert attention-grabbing piece of information]?" Promise: "I will teach you everything the experts know about [insert subject]." Preview: "You'll learn advanced secrets, like [insert tease]."

## QUESTION, QUESTION, QUESTION, PROMISE, PREVIEW

Question: "Did you know that [insert attention–grabbing piece of information]?" Question: "Maybe [insert second attention-grabbing piece of information]?" Question: "How about [insert third attention-grabbing piece of information]?" Promise: "I promise that by the end of this speech, you'll be an expert on [insert subject]." Preview: "You'll even learn hidden, little–known secrets, like [insert tease]."

## BENEFIT QUESTION, PROMISE, PREVIEW

Benefit question: "Do you want [insert benefit]?" Promise: "I will show you how successful [insert type of person] achieve [insert benefit]." Preview: "By [insert tease], you'll even be able to achieve [insert benefit] without [pain point]."

## BENEFIT QUESTION, BENEFIT QUESTION, BENEFIT QUESTION, PROMISE, PREVIEW

Benefit question: "Do you want [insert benefit]?" Benefit question: "How about [insert second benefit]?" Benefit question: "Do you also want to [insert third benefit]?" Promise: "I will show you how successful [insert type of person] achieve [insert first benefit], [insert second benefit], and [insert third benefit]." Preview: "You'll be able to do it by [insert tease]."

## ATTENTION, INTEREST, DESIRE, ACTION

Attention: "[insert attention–grabbing technique]." Interest: "This is something that can help you [insert benefit one], [insert benefit two], and [insert benefit three]." Desire: "It's valuable to you because [insert reason one], [insert reason two], and [insert reason three]." Action: "And if you want it, all you have to do is [insert action]."

## TRUST, KNOW, LIKE

Trust: "I have [insert proof of authority]. I say this not to brag, but just so that you know I'm someone you can trust to help you [insert outcome]." Know: "I am [insert brief autobiography]." Like: "I'm also trying to [insert common goals]. Just like you, I [insert similarity]. You are clearly all [insert compliment] who are more than capable of achieving [insert outcome] with the proper strategies."

## PROBLEM, CONSEQUENCES, SOLUTION

Problem: "You all have a problem: [insert problem]." Consequences: "This problem will [insert consequence one], [insert consequence two], and [insert consequence three]." Solution: "But I'll show you a solution."

## DANGER, AGITATE, SOLUTION

Danger: "This is urgent. We are all in danger. We are all at risk of [insert danger]." Agitate: "This will [insert greater consequences] and make us experience [insert emotional consequences] as [insert greater consequences] happens." Solution: "But we can protect yourselves if you [insert tease of solution]."

## FEAR, RECOMMENDATION, PROOF, BELIEF

Fear: "We are all at risk of [insert danger]. This will [insert negative consequences]." Recommendation: "I recommend that you [insert action] to protect yourselves." Proof: "You can trust this solution because [insert proof]." Belief: "You all have what it takes to [insert action] and save yourselves from [insert fear]. You are all capable. [insert recommendation] can work for you."

## LEAD, INFO GAP, OPEN LOOP

Lead: "[insert your entire message summarized in one sentence]." Information gap: "You all probably believe [insert related common belief]. But the truth is that [insert related common belief] is quite far from the truth. Open loop: "And little do you know, [insert surprising piece of information]. But we'll talk about that later."

## PAIN QUESTION, GUIDE, AUTHORITY, EMPATHY

Pain question: "Are you struggling with [insert pain point]?" Guide: "I can help you." Authority: "I am [insert proof of authority]." Empathy: "I care that you solve [insert pain point] because I remember when I struggled with [insert pain point]. I remember how it felt. I remember feeling [insert emotional consequences]."

## PAIN QUESTION, PAIN QUESTION, PAIN QUESTION, GUIDE, AUTHORITY, EMPATHY

Pain question: "Are you struggling with [insert first pain point]?" Pain question: "Maybe you feel like [insert second pain point]?" Pain question: "All in all, do you struggle with [insert third pain point]?" Guide: "I can help you." Authority: "I am [insert proof of authority]." Empathy: "I care that you solve [insert pain point] because I remember when I struggled with [insert pain point]. I remember how it felt. I remember feeling [insert emotional consequences]."

## TENSION, DESIRE, ATTENTION

Tension: "You might think you are [insert self–identification]. But if you were [insert self–identification], you wouldn't be [insert contradicting fact of reality]." Desire: "Do you want to truly make yourself [insert aspirational self-identification]?" Attention: "I'll teach you how to become [insert aspirational self-identification]."

## CURIOSITY, PROMISE, PREVIEW

Curiosity: "Did you know that [insert attention–grabbing piece of information]?" Promise: "Shortly, I'll explain the little-known truth [attention-grabbing piece of information]." Preview: "It has to do with [insert tease]."

## CURIOSITY, CURIOSITY, CURIOSITY, PROMISE, PREVIEW

Curiosity: "Did you know that [insert attention-grabbing piece of information]?" Curiosity: "What surprises me even more is that [insert more attention-grabbing piece of information]." Curiosity: "And the most surprising part of it all is that [insert the most attention-grabbing piece of information]." Promise: "I have some of the answers." Preview: "They have to do with [insert tease]."

## MOMENT, FUTURE, DECISION

Moment: "Right now, we are [insert negative fact]." Future: "But it's possible for us to have a future where [insert positive outcome]." Decision: "Which do we want? [insert negative fact] or [insert positive outcome in the future]? It's time for us to decide."

## BENEFIT, PAIN POINT, PROOF

Benefit: "I'll teach you how to [insert benefit]." Pain point: "And I'll teach you how to [insert benefit] without having to deal with [insert pain point]." Proof: "This worked for [insert testimonial or other proof]."

## BENEFIT, PAIN POINT, BENEFIT, PAIN POINT, BENEFIT, PAIN POINT, SKEPTICISM, PROOF

Benefit: "I'll teach you how to [insert benefit]." Pain point: "And I'll teach you how to [insert benefit] without having to deal with [insert pain point]." Benefit: "You'll also learn how to [insert second benefit]." Pain point: "And usually [insert second benefit] involves [insert second pain point], but I'll teach you how to avoid that." Benefit: "But the best part is that you'll be able to [insert third benefit]." Pain point: "And unlike most other people, you'll be able to [insert third benefit] without [insert third pain point]." Skepticism: "You're probably questioning this, maybe you're thinking [insert skepticism]." Proof: "But this worked for [insert testimonial or other proof]."

## ASK, EXCHANGE, OUTCOME

Ask: "Want [insert benefit]?" Exchange: "If you give me [number] minutes, I'll teach you how to [insert benefit]." Outcome: "And at the end of it, you'll [insert positive outcome]."

## QUESTION PRESENTATION, TEASE, ANSWER

Question presentation: "The big question everyone is trying to answer is [insert question]." Tease: "Some people even say [insert tease]." Answer: "But I believe I have the big answer, and it's not what any of us expected."

## QUESTION PRESENTATION, TEASE, TEASE, TEASE, ANSWER

Question presentation: "The big question everyone is trying to answer is [insert question]." Tease: "Some people even say [insert tease]." Tease: "There are others who believe that the answer is [insert answer]. They're wrong though." Tease: "Ultimately, nobody really knew the answer until recently. They just knew [insert tease]." Answer: "But I recently discovered what I believe is the answer."

## ANXIETY, AGITATE, PERMISSION

Anxiety: "[insert problem] can create [insert anxiety-inducing consequences]. It's okay to be worried about it." Agitate: "But being worried won't help prevent [insert consequence] caused by [insert problem]." Permission: "If you let me talk to you about this, I'll show you how to solve [insert problem] and escape the worrying about [insert problem]."

## ANXIETY, AGITATE, POSITIVE PERMISSION, HELP

Anxiety: "[insert problem] can create [insert anxiety-inducing consequences]." Agitate: "[insert problem] causes [insert consequence one], [insert consequence two], and [insert consequence three]. You're probably really anxious about this problem – and that's understandable" Positive permission: "Nobody is judging you for that. You don't need anybody's permission to feel anxious about [insert problem]. It is a perfectly legitimate, valid feeling." Help: "Still, I can help you avoid [insert problem]."

---

**KEY INSIGHT:**

## Understanding Rhetorical Formulas Becomes an Obstacles If You Don't Deeply Understand Your Audience. You Risk Using the Wrong Formula In the Wrong Way On the Wrong People At the Wrong Time.

---

## YOU HEARD, THEY SAY, I SAY

You heard: "You may have heard [insert critics or opponents] criticizing [insert subject] – saying [insert criticism one], [criticism two], and [criticism three]. They say [summarize their main objection]. But I say [insert rebuttal that resolves what they say.]"

## YES QUESTION, YES QUESTION, YES QUESTION, MAIN QUESTION

Yes question: "Have you ever wondered [insert common question]?" Yes question: "Do you ever feel like [insert common feeling]? Yes question: "Would you like to [insert positive outcome]?" Main question: "Are you ready to [insert desired action]?"

## EVOKE VALUES, PACE, LEAD

Evoke values: "We believe in [insert shared value]. We hold above all else [insert second shared value]. And we seek [insert third shared value]." Pacing: "[describe ways in which your worldview resembles that of your audience members.]" Leading: "[slowly transition into changing their worldview and doing so gently.]"

## PREDICTION, JUSTIFICATION, PREVIEW

Prediction: "In the next [insert timeframe], [insert occurrence] will happen." Justification: "Why? Because [insert brief reason]." Preview: "I will explain why [insert brief reason] will cause [insert occurrence], what we can do about it, and what it means for you."

## SECRET, PROMISE, PREVIEW

Secret: "There's a hidden, little-known secret of [insert subject]." Promise: "I will pull back the veil and show you this hidden truth of [insert subject]." Preview: "It is surprising because it has to do with [insert tease]."

## SECRET, BENEFIT, PROMISE, PREVIEW

Secret: "There's a hidden, little-known secret of [insert subject]." Benefit: "This secret allows us to [insert benefit] and achieve [insert positive outcome]. Promise: "I will pull back the veil and show you this hidden truth of [insert subject]." Preview: "It is surprising because it has to do with [insert tease]."

## INFO GAP, INFO GAP, INFO GAP

Information gap: "Chances are you believe [insert common belief]. This is partly true, but it misses an essential aspect of [insert subject]." Information gap: "And if you believe [insert second common belief], you're also missing something subtle but important." Information gap: "The brutal truth is that even [insert third common belief] doesn't fully represent the truth. More is going on than meets the eye."

## OPEN LOOP, OPEN LOOP, OPEN LOOP

Open loop: "There's a little-known process that can [insert benefit]." Open loop: "We are even able to use this process to [insert second benefit]." Open loop: "But the best part is that we can [insert third benefit] without [insert pain point]."

## QUESTION, BIG ANSWER, TEASE

Question: "Why does [insert occurrence] happen?" Big answer: "There's a little-known reason nobody is talking about." Tease: "It has to do with [insert tease]."

## GAIN, LOGIC, FEAR

Gain: "We can [insert gain]." Logic: "We can [insert gain] because [insert logical support]." Fear: "But time is running out. The longer we wait, the more likely we are to miss the opportunity to [insert gain]. Let me explain..."

## ATTENTION, NEED, SATISFACTION, VISUALIZATION, ACTION

Attention: "Hey! Listen to me, you have a problem!" Need: "Let me explain the problem." Satisfaction: "But, I have a solution!" Visualization: "If we implement my solution, this is what will happen. Or, if we don't implement my solution, this is what will happen." Action: "You can help me in this specific way. Will you help me?"

## ACCUSATION, RELIEF, SOLUTION

Accusation: "We [insert negative behavior]." Relief: "But it's okay. We can get through this." Solution: "We can solve [insert negative behavior] with [insert solution]."

## ACCUSATION, ACCUSATION, ACCUSATION, RELIEF, SOLUTION

Accusation: "We [insert negative behavior]." Accusation: "And even though we know we shouldn't, we also [insert second negative behavior]." Accusation: "But the worst yet is that we [insert third negative behavior]." Relief: "We face a difficult challenge to grapple with." Solution: "Still, we can solve [insert negative behavior], [insert negative behavior two], and [insert negative behavior three], with [insert solution]."

## PAST, PRESENT, MEANS

Past: "I used to struggle with [insert subject]. It used to make me feel [insert negative emotions]. My biggest problem was [insert biggest problem]. Maybe you can relate to this." Present: "Now, I excel at [insert subject] with ease. It makes me feel [insert positive emotions]. I solved [insert biggest problem] and it made everything so much easier." Means: "Let me tell you exactly how I did this, going from [insert negative past] to [insert positive present]."

## WON'T GIVE, WILL GIVE, WHY

Won't give: "I won't give you [insert negative type of speech]." Will give: "Instead, I'll give you [insert positive type of speech]." Why: "Why? Because that's exactly what you deserve, and because [insert moral reason]."

## DESIRE, METHODS

Desire: "Want to satisfy [insert basic human desire]?" Methods: "Here's how..."

## OLD PLAN, JUSTIFICATION, DECISION, JUSTIFICATION, NEW PLAN

Old plan: "Coming here, I planned on giving you [insert negative or suboptimal type of speech, like 'a watered-down version of the truth']." Justification: "I was going to do this because [insert justification, like 'you are first-year economic students and this is extremely complicated.'] Decision: "Then I decided I wasn't going to do that." Justification: "The reason being that [insert justification for decision, like 'it's challenging, but it is essential to understand for the well-being of our economy, and from what I heard, you are all bright and attentive, so you can handle it.']" New plan: "So instead, I'm going to give you [insert positive type of speech, like 'the difficult, nuanced, messy truth of the situation']."

## BAD PATH, GOOD PATH, CHALLENGE

Bad path: "Right now, we could make the mistake of [insert bad path]." Good path: "Or, we could do the right thing and [insert good path]." Challenge: "Which will it be? I challenge us to do the right thing and [insert good path]."

## FAILURE, SUCCESS, ATTENTION

Failure: "We can fail at [insert endeavor] and experience [insert consequence]." Success: "Or, we can succeed at [insert endeavor], and experience [insert benefit]." Attention: "I would like to share a way to tip the scales in our favor, guaranteeing success in [insert endeavor]."

## THREAT, CONSEQUENCE, ATTENTION

Threat: "We are under attack from [insert threat]." Consequence: "We are at risk of [insert consequence]." Attention: "I know how we can protect ourselves."

## NEGATIVITY, AVOIDANCE, ATTENTION

Negativity: "We have gone through a lot with [describe negative experiences]." Avoidance: "Yes: this has happened in the past, but it doesn't have to be our future. We can avoid [insert negative experiences]." Attention: "I would like to tell you how."

## CHARACTER, PROBLEM, PLAN, SUCCESS

Character: "I help [insert type of person]..." Problem: "Overcome [insert problem]..." Plan: "With [insert plan]..." Success: "So that they can [insert vision of success]..."

## OUTCOME, MINUS PAIN POINT

Outcome: "We can [insert positive outcome]." Minus pain point: "And we can do it without [insert pain point]."

## OUTCOME, MINUS PAIN POINT, MINUS PAIN POINT, MINUS PAIN POINT

Outcome: "We can [insert positive outcome]." Minus pain point: "We can do it without [insert pain point]." Minus pain point: "We can do it without [insert second pain point]." Minus pain point: "But the best part is that we can achieve [insert original positive outcome] without [insert third and worst pain point]."

## WANT BENEFIT, MEANS

Want benefit: "If we want [insert benefit]..." Means: "Here's how we can attain it: [insert means to achieve benefit]."

## WANT BENEFIT, WANT BENEFIT, WANT BENEFIT, MEANS

Want benefit: "Want [insert benefit]?" Want benefit: "Want [insert second benefit]?" Want benefit: "Want [insert third benefit]?" Means: "Here's how we can attain it: [insert means to achieve benefits]."

## BACK TO THE BASICS

Let us briefly review the components of effective openings before getting into part two: keeping attention.

## HOW DO YOU WRITE A GOOD INTRODUCTION FOR A SPEECH?

Here are the basic guidelines: Start with an attention-grabbing opening, not a personal introduction. Maximize information scent. Use crisp, commanding phrases. Start with controlled energy. Layer on the benefits early: benefits sell. Start with one of the preceding openings or formulas. Consider using interaction. Focus on novelty: people love new information. Keep it simple. Choose the right speech opening for the occasion.

### KEY INSIGHT:

# Using Rhetorical Formulas Demands Both Adherence and Adaptation.

# You Must Adhere to the Formula You Choose to Execute, But Also Adapt It to Your Audience, Your Subject, And Your Speaking Style.

## HOW DO YOU START A SPEECH IN A UNIQUE AND EFFECTIVE WAY?

Most speakers make the mistake of starting with a personal introduction. Instead, you should start with an attention-grabbing opening (like I've taught you). Remember that your audience is going through a mental checklist trying to answer the question: "should I listen to this?"

## HOW DO YOU START YOUR PERSONAL INTRODUCTION?

In a way that is relevant to your subject. A powerful technique is to weave your personal details into the speech opening. That way, you guarantee that the personal introduction is relevant. You also guarantee that your audience is paying attention.

## ADVANCED TECHNIQUES

In this section, you're going to learn the advanced techniques that will greatly expand your understanding of opening communication with impact. Specifically, you will learn how to make opening formulas, how to shorten and lengthen them, and how to use them at any point in your speech.

## HOW TO MAKE OPENING FORMULAS

Remember all those speech opening formulas? APP? OPP? CPPS? All 54 of them? You can make your own. Those were just the ones that I've identified as particularly powerful. What follows is a list of some (of the many) basic ingredients. Promise: make a promise. Preview: preview your content. Attention: subtly ask for attention. Open loop: create an unclosed curiosity loop. Information gap: poke a hole in audience information. Outcome: explain a positive outcome. Benefit: offer the audience a benefit. Question: ask a rhetorical question. Secret: tease a big secret. Problem: explain an audience problem. Solution: propose a solution to a problem

You can stack these blocks in whatever way you want, and these are not the only blocks. You can also mesh the formulas with the openings that I taught you before. So, combine these openings with each other, and with the strategies that are not formulas, if you want. In short, you can make your own speech opening formulas, suited to whatever purpose you need. And to reiterate, you can also stack the speech opening strategies (things like quotes, startling statistics, and loss warnings). The end result? Powerful speech openings designed by you, specifically for you.

### CREATING YOUR OWN TOWER OF CAPTIVATING SPEECH

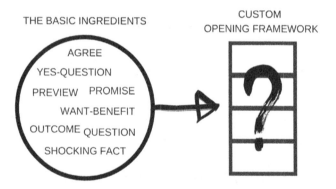

FIGURE 35: You can stack the basic ingredients of these frameworks into a unique, custom opening framework. You can also stack the frameworks themselves into a tower of frameworks. Most high-stakes speeches by U.S. Presidents and other world-leaders had "stacked" openings, using multiple opening strategies in sequence.

## HOW TO SHORTEN AND LENGTHEN OPENINGS

Let's say you are giving a three-minute talk. You need a speech opening, but you don't want a long one. What about a 30-minute talk? You need a robust opening. Here's how you can achieve that: by lengthening and shortening. These formulas and speech opening strategies can be stretched while maintaining a proportional impact.

For example, the APP method can be stretched to this: Agree: "I agree that [insert problem] is frustrating. It makes you feel [insert negative emotions]. I know exactly what it's like. It causes [insert consequences]. I've been dealing with those consequences for a long time." Promise: "But there's an easy solution. Once I found this solution, I was shocked. It's so simple but so powerful. You'll enjoy learning it." Preview: "This solution involves [insert preview]. It also uses [insert preview]. The best part is that [insert preview] makes it much more effective." Both work. These models act as accordions. You can stretch them out, shorten them, or stack them.

**THESE OPENINGS SHORTEN AND EXTEND LIKE ACCORDIONS**

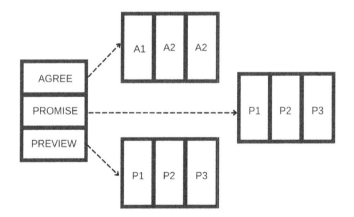

FIGURE 36: You can break down each step into a sequence of statements designed to fulfill it, lengthening that sequence of statements at will. This intensifies the impact of the opening.

## HOW TO USE THEM AT ANY POINT

These models work as speech openings. But you can also sprinkle them at any point throughout your speech. You can use them in these situations, for example: Starting a new idea. Moving to a new part of a speech structure. When you want to regain audience attention during a difficult, information-dense segment.

### USE THESE FORMULAS AS UNIVERSAL HOOKS

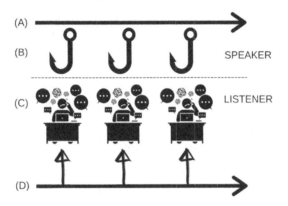

FIGURE 37: As you are delivering your speech (A), you will need to throw at multiple hooks (B) to fight the distractions (C) the listener's internal dialogue is sending them (D). These opening frameworks can act as those hooks.

..................................Chapter Summary................................

- Some of these opening models simply ask that you present a particular idea or theme first.
- Other opening models are full-fledged, step-by-step formulas that you can fill in with your meaning.
- You can stack these opening structures, using them in a sequence for an even greater attention-grabbing pull.

- The goal of these openings is to maximize curiosity, impact, and intrigue within the first eight seconds.
- The first goal of a speech is to grab audience attention in a relevant and fitting manner.
- These opening formulas are all designed specifically to achieve that goal – specifically to grab attention.

---

**KEY INSIGHT:**

Our Nervous Systems Take in an Incalculable Number of Inputs, Consciously and Unconsciously.

Judgment is the Result of Reason Acting On These Inputs, As Well As Past (And Anticipated) Inputs.

---

Email Peter D. Andrei, the author of the Speak for Success collection and the President of Speak Truth Well LLC directly.

pandreibusiness@gmail.com

## GRABBING, KEEPING, DIRECTING ATTENTION (PART ONE)

| 1 | Grabbing Attention |
|---|---|
| 1.1 | Openings Are Make-or-Break Moments |
| 1.2 | Present a Personal Introduction After Grabbing Attention |
| 1.3 | Start with the Hook Before Your Personal Introduction |
| 1.4 | Recognize and Appeal to the Information-Foraging Dynamic |
| 1.5 | Maximize Information Scent Early on to Grab Attention |
| 1.6 | Speak with Crisp, Commanding Phrases to Drop Cognitive Load |
| 1.7 | Don't Stuff Your Sentences: One Idea Per Sentence at First |
| 1.8 | Begin with Fast Pace, High Energy, and Appropriate Intensity |
| 1.9 | Successfully Convey Value and Draw Interest in 15 Seconds |
| 1.10 | Master Openings: 20% of the Effort Produces 80% of the Results |
| 1.11 | Create Your Own Opening Formulas By Recombining the Steps |
| 1.12 | Shorten and Lengthen the Frameworks Like an Accordion |
| 1.13 | Use The Openings at Any Point to Regain and Strengthen Attention |
| 2 | Keeping Attention |
| 3 | Directing Attention |

# YOU CAN STACK DIFFERENT TYPES OF HOOKS TOGETHER IN A SEQUENCE

## ASK A QUESTION

How many of you think you know the biggest threat facing our country?

## BREAK A BELIEF

You're wrong if you're thinking national debt, global adversaries, or any of the usual suspects.

## PRESENT SECRECY

It's a threat from within, underlying all threats, hidden in plain sight, lurking yet obvious.

**Claim These Free Resources that Will Help You Unleash the Power of Your Words and Speak with Confidence. Visit www.speakforsuccesshub.com/toolkit for Access.**

### 18 Free PDF Resources

*12 Iron Rules for Captivating Story, 21 Speeches that Changed the World, 341-Point Influence Checklist, 143 Persuasive Cognitive Biases, 17 Ways to Think On Your Feet, 18 Lies About Speaking Well, 137 Deadly Logical Fallacies, 12 Iron Rules For Captivating Slides, 371 Words that Persuade, 63 Truths of Speaking Well, 27 Laws of Empathy, 21 Secrets of Legendary Speeches, 19 Scripts that Persuade, 12 Iron Rules For Captivating Speech, 33 Laws of Charisma, 11 Influence Formulas, 219-Point Speech-Writing Checklist, 21 Eloquence Formulas*

**Claim These Free Resources that Will Help You Unleash
the Power of Your Words and Speak with Confidence. Visit
www.speakforsuccesshub.com/toolkit for Access.**

### 30 Free Video Lessons

We'll send you one free video lesson every day for 30 days, written
and recorded by Peter D. Andrei. Days 1-10 cover authenticity, the
prerequisite to confidence and persuasive power. Days 11-20 cover
building self-belief and defeating communication anxiety. Days 21-30
cover how to speak with impact and influence, ensuring your words
change minds instead of falling flat. Authenticity, self-belief, and
impact – this course helps you master three components of
confidence, turning even the most high-stakes presentations from
obstacles into opportunities.

**Claim These Free Resources that Will Help You Unleash the Power of Your Words and Speak with Confidence. Visit www.speakforsuccesshub.com/toolkit for Access.**

**2 Free Workbooks**

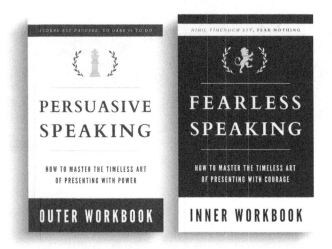

We'll send you two free workbooks, including long-lost excerpts by Dale Carnegie, the mega-bestselling author of *How to Win Friends and Influence People* (5,000,000 copies sold). *Fearless Speaking* guides you in the proven principles of mastering your inner game as a speaker. *Persuasive Speaking* guides you in the time-tested tactics of mastering your outer game by maximizing the power of your words. All of these resources complement the Speak for Success collection.

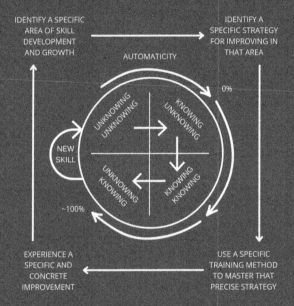

How do anxious speakers turn into articulate masters of the craft? Here's how: With the bulletproof, scientifically-proven, 2,500-year-old (but mostly forgotten) process pictured above.

First, we identify a specific area of improvement. Perhaps your body language weakens your connection with the audience. At this point, you experience "unknowing unknowing." You don't know you don't know the strategy you will soon learn for improving in this area.

Second, we choose a specific strategy for improving in this area. Perhaps we choose "open gestures," a type of gesturing that draws the audience in and holds attention.

At this point, you experience "knowing unknowing." You know you don't know the strategy. Your automaticity, or how automatically you perform the strategy when speaking, is 0%.

Third, we choose a specific drill or training method to help you practice open gestures. Perhaps you give practice speeches and perform the gestures. At this point, you experience "knowing knowing." You know you know the strategy.

And through practice, you formed a weak habit, so your automaticity is somewhere between 0% and 100%.

Fourth, you continue practicing the technique. You shift into "unknowing knowing." You forgot you use this type of gesture, because it became a matter of automatic habit. Your automaticity is 100%.

And just like that, you've experienced a significant and concrete improvement. You've left behind a weakness in communication and gained a strength. Forever. Every time you speak, you use this type of gesture, and you do it without even thinking about it. This alone can make the difference between a successful and unsuccessful speech.

Now repeat. Master a new skill. Create a new habit. Improve in a new area. How else could we improve your body language? What about the structure of your communication? Your persuasive strategy? Your debate skill? Your vocal modulation? With this process, people gain measurable and significant improvements in as little as one hour. Imagine if you stuck with it over time. This is the path to mastery. This is the path to unleashing the power of your words.

**Access your 18 free PDF resources, 30 free video lessons, and 2 free workbooks from this link: www.speakforsuccesshub.com/toolkit**

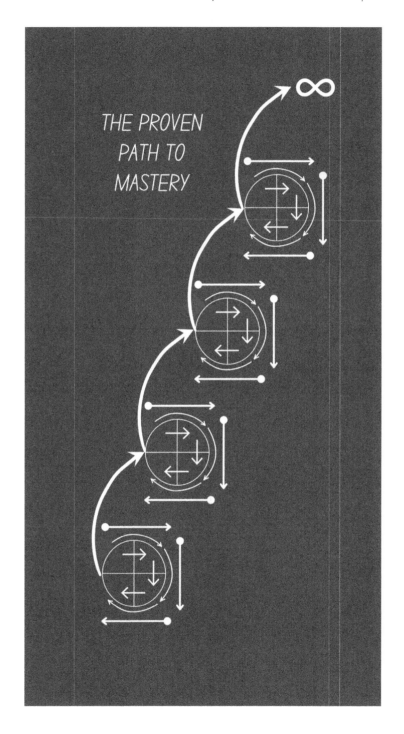

THE PROVEN
PATH TO
MASTERY

**SPEAK FOR SUCCESS COLLECTION BOOK**

# XIV

**THE PSYCHOLOGY OF COMMUNICATION CHAPTER**

# III

# THE MIDDLE:
## Keeping Attention

## SPEECH TRANSITIONS: TRANSFERING ATTENTION FROM POINT TO POINT

I F YOU DON'T USE SPEECH TRANSITIONS, YOUR SPEECHES might confuse your audiences, make little sense, and confuse *you.* In this chapter, you will learn exactly how to use speech transitions to make sure that your audience enjoys listening to you, your speeches sound eloquent, and your words are clear and powerful. Further, using these transitions will ensure that you keep the attention you earned with your openings, ensuring you don't lose it throughout the rest of the message.

## UNDERSTANDING THE BASICS OF SPEECH TRANSITIONS

If you don't understand the basics of speech transitions, you won't be able to master them. And if you can't master speech transitions, public speaking will be much harder.

## WHAT ARE SOME EXAMPLES OF TRANSITION WORDS?

Transition words are transition phrases that are single words. Transition words are snappier, shorter, and quicker than transition phrases. They heighten the pace and intensity of a sentence in a speech. Some examples are: "Instead," "Additionally," "Also," "Next," "Now," "And," "Lastly," "First," "Because," "Since," etc. They work because they are, essentially, a mini open-loop. When you connect one sentence to another by starting the second with the word "but," that implies an exception to an aforementioned rule, for example. And people are captivated by that mini open-loop because they want to complete it. "But... *what?*" Technically, all transitions are mini open-loops until the sentence is finished (or until it reveals the resolution to the implicit open loop), but these are particularly effective because they are just one word.

## WHY ARE TRANSITIONS IMPORTANT IN A SPEECH?

Transitions are important in a speech because they smooth the flow of information. Transitions also show the audience what is coming next. They connect what you are about to say with what you just said. Transitions guarantee eloquence. They help your audience understand each of your sentences as they relate to each other, forming a coherent, smooth, flowing message instead of a stilted one.

### TRANSITIONS SERVE AN INVALUABLE FUNCTION

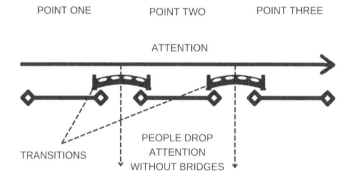

FIGURE 38: Moving from point one to two to three and bridging the points with transitions carries attention across. The vertical dotted arrows reveal the path of attention without the transitions: slipping away from your points through the cracks between points – cracks that the transitions fill. Build bridges to close the gaps between points, so attention doesn't leak out through the. This is the essence of transitioning. The greater the gap, the bigger the bridge. We will revisit this with the "transition map" principle revealed at the end of this section.

## WHAT ARE THE THREE TYPES OF TRANSITIONS?

Funny… I made this section "what are the three types of transitions" because thousands of people have been typing this in Google, according to a tool of mine that shows search engine trends. Here's the funny part: there aren't *three* types of transitions. There are over 60. Which type of transition you choose depends on the relationship between your previous sentence and your next one. Choose the type of transition that acts as a gateway into your next sentence.

## HOW DO YOU WRITE A GOOD TRANSITION?

You write a good transition by choosing a transition that's not already been used excessively in your message, that's clear, and that's relevant to your speech. You write a good transition by shortening transition phrases to get rid of unnecessary words. You write a good transition by connecting your previous sentence to your next one. That's the key idea here.

### ANSWER THIS CRITICAL QUESTION TO CAPTURE ATTENTION

FIGURE 39: What links what I just said to what I am about to say? What bridges what I just said to what I am about to say? Answer this question to find your transition.

## WHAT ARE SOME GOOD TRANSITION PHRASES?

What is a good transition word? That depends on what you want to say. Good transition phrases connect your previous sentence to your next sentence. If your next sentence will describe something different then your last one, "On the contrary..." is a good transition. "Similarly..." is obviously not a good one.

## HOW DO YOU INTRODUCE A MAIN POINT IN A SPEECH?

You introduce a main point in a speech by using a transition of importance. A transition of importance indicates that what you are about to say is your main point. It shows the audience that it is your main message. Here are some examples: "the whole point is," "and here's what this all means," etc.

## 48 BASIC TYPES OF SPEECH TRANSITIONS (288 EXAMPLES)

This section will teach you exactly how to use speech transitions. You'll learn 48 proven speech transitions that will make your words flow like a river.

## DIFFERENCE

These indicate that what you are about to say is different from what you just said. Use these to indicate contrasts, and to prime your audience to identify differences. "On the contrary..." "Unlike..." "As opposed to..." "Conversely..." "On the other hand..." "If we flip that around..."

## SIMILARITY

These indicate that what you are about to say is similar to what you just said. These will prime your audience to identify similar characteristics. Use these for metaphors, similes, and analogies. "Similarly..." "Just like..." "This is a lot like..." "Something similar is..." "This mirrors the..." "Much like..."

## SPECIFICATION

These elaborate upon a previous point. Use these when you're diving deeper into an idea. Use these when you want to present additional information about an idea. "Additionally..." "Furthermore..." "To elaborate..." "Also..." "There's more..." "It goes deeper..."

## LIST ITEMS

These present the items in a list of items. A sequence of these transitions is efficient and memorable. Your audience will remember content that's structured in a list. One tip: don't say "lastly..." say "last." Don't say "firstly..." say "first." There's no need for the "ly." "First..." "Second..." "Third..." "Fourth..." "Fifth..." "Last..."

## CHRONOLOGY

These present a list of events in chronological sequence. Chronologies are naturally engaging. People love stories. Use these to build a rapid, fast-paced chronology. "Next..." "Then..." "After this..." "What happened next..." "Now..." "The next thing..."

## CLOSING

These indicate that you are closing your speech. Often, your audience will lose attention in the middle of your speech. People love listening to the beginning and ending of a speech, but lose attention in the middle. Use these transitions to bring back some of those people. "To conclude…" "Before I close…" "Bringing this to an end…" "I want to tell you one last thing…" "So, if you remember one thing from this speech before I close…" "Here are my parting words…"

## REFERRAL

These are used to refer back to a previous point. You'll often find that certain parts of your speech are especially relevant. You'll often find that you need to constantly return to those points. Use these transitions to do so. "As I said…" "If you recall…" "Like I mentioned previously…" "Earlier, I said that…" "Remember when I said…" "Just as I said before…"

## OPENINGS

These are used to open your speech, or part of your speech – perhaps moving from the opening itself to your first point. They signal to your audience that it's time to pay close attention. "Today, we'll be talking about…" "Here's what you'll learn today…" "The first point I want to make is…" "To start…" "Let's begin…" "Here's what I want to tell you first…"

## CAUSE AND EFFECT

These present the impact of a cause. It's always important to elaborate on a cause. So, if you say something like "20% of kids are disengaged in schools," elaborate on the impact of that with these transitions. "The consequence is that…" "Because of this…" "This results in…" "This leads to…" "Due to this…" "This causes…"

## EXAMPLES

These present an example. The more examples you give, the more convincing you'll be. Use these to make sure your audience understands you're giving an example. "For example..." "An example of this is..." "Such as..." "This is shown by..." "A clear sign of this..." "A perfect example is..."

## QUOTATIONS

These present a quotation by another speaker. If you can borrow famous quotes, you gain instant eloquence. You also support your stance. That's why quotes are rhetorically powerful. "It was once said by [person]..." "To quote [person]..." "[person] once said..." "According to [person]..." "A great quote about this subject is when [person] said..." "[person] famously said that..."

**KEY INSIGHT:**

Using the Wise Words of Wise People Is Itself an Act of Wisdom.

Quote the People Who Embody the Relevant Human Aspirations; If You Speak of Courage, Quote Someone Brave.

## SECTION SUMMARIES

These summarize previous points. It's important to repeat your points. This will help your audience remember them. Use these transitions to indicate summaries: "To summarize..." "So far, the big idea is..." "What this all means is..." "To put it simply..." "To quickly restate it..." "The main point is..."

## SPEECH SUMMARIES

These summarize entire speeches. It's always a good idea to remind your audience what they just learned. It helps cement the content in their long-term memory. Use these transitions to make the summary clear: "After listening, I hope you learned..." "Today, we discussed..." "In this speech, we explored..." "Here's exactly what you learned today..." "To restate what we talked about..." "Here's what you should remember from this speech..."

## DEMONSTRATIONS

These transition to demonstrations. Speakers who include demonstrations often confuse their audiences. These transitions will make it clear that a demonstration is actually going on. "And if you turn your attention to..." "I'll demonstrate this..." "This will demonstrate what we were talking about..." "Look at this demonstration..." "This demonstration will show you..." "Here's a quick demonstration..."

## ANOTHER SPEAKER

These transition to another speaker. They make it clear that you're handing it off to someone else. "It's my pleasure to introduce..." "I'm honored to introduce..." "Someone has more to say..." "Now [person's name] is going to say a few words to you..." "It's time to hear from..." "Thanks for listening. Up next, is..."

## CORE ISSUE

These transition to a core problem or central idea. Use these to indicate that what you're about to say is of special importance. "The core issue is..." "What this all means is..." "The central problem is..." "When we boil it down..." "In a sentence, the fundamental problem is..." "So, if we talk about what's really going on..."

## OPPOSING POINTS

These transition to an opposite stance. Imagine not using these transitions. Your audience would think you just contradicted yourself. "Those who disagree say..." "The opposite stance is..." "The main counter-argument is..." "My opponents say..." "The common disagreement is..." "Unfortunately, many critics say..."

## IMPORTANCE

These transitions move to an important idea. Audience attention ebbs and flows. It increases and decreases. To get it back, use an importance transition. "The most important idea is..." "The significant part is..." "This is the most important part..." "Let's get to the crucial part..." "The single biggest idea is..." "Here's the important part..."

## ANECDOTES

These transition to a personal anecdote. Personal anecdotes are effective because they build audience relatability. They strengthen the speaker to audience connection. But you have to open them up with the proper transition. "And I have a personal story that..." "The other day..." "There's a story that..." "There's a funny story..." "One time, I was..." "I have a perfect story for this..."

## VISUAL AIDS

These transition to a visual aid. Visual aids are useful because they back up verbal information with visual information. But you need to make sure that your audience actually looks at the visual. How? With these transitions. "If you turn your attention to..." "As you can see on the whiteboard..." "This chart indicates..." "I've put together this visual..." "This PowerPoint slide..." "Look here to see..."

## ACTION

These transition to your call to action. Your speech needs a call to action to create real-world impact. And if you transition to it, your audience will pay attention, and then actually take action. "Here's how you can help me..." "Want to take action?" "You can change this by..." "Here's what you can do..." "It's time to take action and..." "Your opportunity to act is..."

## CONCURRENCE

These transitions indicate that two things are happening at the same time. If you ever want to show concurrence, you have to use these transitions. Otherwise, your audience won't understand it. "At the same time..." "While..." "During this..." "Concurrently..." "As this was happening..." "At the same exact moment..."

## CONTINUATION

These transitions indicate that something is continuing. If you want to present something, and then take it a step further, use these transitions. "And it continues to..." "It goes on to..." "It doesn't end there, but..." "It keeps going..." "Did you think it was over?" "It doesn't stop just yet, but..."

## EXCEPTION

These transitions indicate an exception to a rule. Always enumerate exceptions as a public speaker. Why? It's the honest thing to do. Seldom do rules exist without exception. "Except for..." "In all cases but..." "But not if..." "Unless..." "Usually, but not if..." "It doesn't happen if..."

## QUALIFICATION

These transitions indicate the specific circumstances in which something happens. They qualify your statements to specific circumstances. "Only if..." "Unless..." "Only in these exact circumstances..." "Specifically when..." "Only when..." "But only in the following conditions..."

## DESPITE

These transitions indicate that something happens despite something else. They show the audience that the two things usually contradict, and can't happen together. "Even though..." "Despite this..." "This happens even while..." "And yet..." "Although..." "Nevertheless..."

## EVIDENCE

These transitions indicate that evidence is about to be presented. Presenting evidence is persuasive and convincing. Presenting evidence with an evidence transition is even better. Why? It commands the audience's attention towards the evidence. "This is

proven by..." "The proof is that..." "I'll show you the evidence..."
"For example..." "As evidence..." "The evidence is that..."

## CENTRAL MESSAGE

These transitions indicate the presentation of the central message.
Almost all speeches are centered around one big idea. It's always a
good idea to explicitly state this idea. When you do, make sure to use
a central message transition. "And the fundamental idea is that..."
"This all comes down to..." "The most important idea is that..."
"Ultimately..." "The whole point is that..." "As you can see, one core
truth emerges..."

---

KEY INSIGHT:

Every Speech Must Be About
One Idea. Any Other Ideas Must
Be There Only to Support the
Main Message.

We Have Weak Memory. If You
Get Someone to Remember Just
One Big Idea, You Won.

---

## PROBLEM

These transitions indicate a problem. You're often speaking to solve a problem. Specifically state the problem, and when you do, use these transitions. "The problem is that..." "The reason it doesn't work is..." "The issue is that..." "Unfortunately, something goes wrong, specifically..." "It doesn't work because..." "But there's a problem..."

## SOLUTION

These transitions indicate a solution. Stating a problem is great, but you have to also present a solution. To make sure everyone hears your solution, introduce it with one of these transitions. "Here's how we can solve it..." "To fix it, we have to..." "It's easy to fix if we..." "Luckily, there's an easy solution..." "The solution is to..." "All we have to do to solve it is..."

## POSITIVE EQUATION

This equation indicates that something is equal to something else. Use these when you're presenting metaphors, similes, or analogies. Use these when you're presenting logical syllogisms ($A = B = C$, so $A = C$). "It is..." "This means..." "It's the same thing as..." "It's equivalent to..." "It's the exact same thing as..." "It is a form of..."

## NEGATIVE EQUATION

This indicates that something isn't equal to something else. Use these especially when people assume two different things are the same. Break that false assumption with these transitions. "It's not..." "It doesn't mean..." "It's not the same thing as..." "It's not equivalent to..." "It's the exact opposite of..." "It's not a form of..."

## OPTIONS

This indicates that what you're going to say next is one of multiple options. Use this when you're trying to navigate a set of possible actions. "One choice is..." "Or, we could..." "An option is to..." "One thing we could do..." "One possible solution is..." "One course of action is..."

## SEQUENCE

This indicates a sequential narrative. Sequential narratives are engaging. Audiences love them. If you want to make your sequential narrative clear, use these transitions. "This leads to..." "After this, what happens is..." "This causes..." "The next step is always..." "What happens next is that..." "The next thing that happens is..."

## OUTLINE

These transitions present an outline. Outlines are effective because they mentally prime your audience members to receive the information that's coming next. It helps them see how it all fits together. You can do outlines of what you've already discussed, or outlines of what's coming next. Regardless, use these transitions when you do. "The big ideas are..." "You'll learn..." "So far, you've learned..." "The three main concepts we talked about are..." "This is what we've discussed so far..." "I'll teach you these three key concepts..."

## INTENSIFICATION

These intensify statements. If you are building up intensity, and you want to continue that, use these. They increase the magnitude of the quality of your subject. Your subject becomes more of whatever you said it was (good, bad, funny, etc.) "But it gets worse..." "It's even more extreme..." "It's worse than it seems..." "It gets better..." "I'll tell you why it's even better..." "Just wait, it gets crazier..."

## MINIMIZATION

These minimize statements. If you want to decrease the intensity, use these. "But that's pretty much it..." "Luckily, it ends when..." "It doesn't move past..." "That's all it is..." "That's about it..." "There's not much else..."

## DIRECTION

These indicate statements about the direction of things. People care more about where things are going then where they are. "We're going to..." "It's moving towards..." "It's going the way of..." "We're moving in a direction of..." "The way we're going will..." "We're taking the route towards..."

## DESTINATION

These indicate what the end result of something is. If you are making forecasts into the future, use these transitions. "We'll end up..." "It's going to become..." "The end result will be..." "It's all going to lead us to..." "At the end of it, we'll end up..." "It's going to result in..."

## SCALE

These indicate a shift in scale. When you use these transitions, you're identifying whether the following subject is huge, or insignificant but worth mentioning. "It's huge..." "It's no big deal, but..." "A massive breakthrough is..." "It's small but..." "This immense innovation is..." "It's insignificant, but..."

### REASON

These indicate that you are going to describe a reason. Often, you need to diagnose the reasons why something is happening. Use these transitions to grab attention right before you present your findings. "The reason why is that..." "Because..." "This happens since..." "Due to the fact that..." "And because of..." "Since..."

### QUALITY

These indicate the quality of the following sentence. They tell your audience how to feel about your upcoming words. This gives you control over audience perception. "It's unbelievable that..." "It's amazing that..." "Unfortunately..." "Luckily for us..." "Thankfully..." "It's sad, but..."

---

**KEY INSIGHT:**

Audiences Subtly Mirror the Salient Speaker they Perceive.

Your Responsibility Is to Portray the Virtues and Emotions You Want Them to Emulate, And to Do So By Showing, Not Telling.

---

## BODY

These indicate that you are moving into the body of your speech. They prime your audience to get ready for the real information. Use them after your opening and introduction as a gateway into your speech. "Let's start..." "To begin..." "Let's get right into it..." "The first point I want to make is that..." "Let's get into our main points..." "First, let's talk about..."

## EXPLANATION

These indicate that you are moving into an explanation. They grab your audience's attention. They prime your audience to closely analyze the explanation. If your audience is confused, this keeps them from tuning out in frustration by telling them you'll simplify it. "But it makes sense when..." "Let me explain..." "But there's an explanation..." "Here's an explanation..." "If you're wondering why, here's the explanation..." "The explanation is..."

## REPETITION

These indicate that you are repeating a previous idea. Moderate repetition is good. It helps audiences remember concepts. It also allows you to reference previous concepts if needed. And it places strategic, rhetorical emphasis on what you're repeating. "To restate..." "Once again..." "I repeat..." "Let me reiterate..." "I'll say it again..." "It's worth mentioning again that..."

## OPINION

These indicate that you are transitioning to a personal opinion. It's important to let your audience know what is verified fact and personal opinion. This is especially true when you move from verified fact to opinion. That's when you need to use one of these transitions.

"Personally, I believe that..." "It's my opinion that..." "I think that..." "In my belief..." "It is my view that..." "If you ask me..."

## QUESTION

These indicate a question or area of intellectual exploration. It's intriguing and builds audience rapport. You can pose a question, and then answer it. Regardless, when transitioning to questions, use one of these. "So, my question is..." "The question we still haven't answered is..." "We still don't know why..." "The big question with no answer is..." "The last unanswered question is..." "The question we need to answer is..."

## PREDICTION

This indicates that what you are about to say is a prediction. And if you are an expert, predictions are good. Just make sure that you use these transitions. "I predict that..." "Here's what's going to happen next, in my view..." "Based on my experience, the next step will be..." "What usually happens next at this point is..." "Next..." "This is what I think will happen next..."

## 23 ADVANCED TRANSITIONS THAT GRAB ATTENTION

These transitions are specifically engineered not only to move from point to point but to do so in a way that reengages the audience.

## REVIEW AND PREVIEW

This reviews what you just said and previews what you're about to say. This is the perfect transition between structural units of speeches. For example, consider a simple speech structure: the problem-solution structure. Right when you finish up the problem section and move into the solution, you can use the review-preview transition like this: "So far, we've talked about the problem. We've discussed how it [insert consequence of problem one, two, and three]. Now, it's time to discuss the solution. We'll talk about how this solution [insert benefits one, two, and three]." Simple, but elegant. It acts as a turning point in your speech. Let's move on to the next advanced speech transition.

**HOW TO SPEAK WITH CLARITY AND DRAW PEOPLE IN**

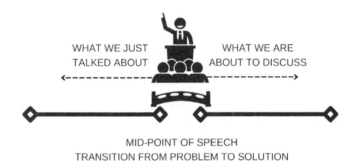

FIGURE 40: Transition by reviewing what you just discussed and previewing what you are about to discuss.

## THEMED TRANSITIONS

Let's say that you want your speech to be unified around a theme. You can use themed transitions. Here's how: identify your theme. Summarize that theme in a word. Inject that word into your transitions. Here's an example: let's say your theme is the "human journey through difficult times and dangerous obstacles." Summarize the theme in one word: "journey." Inject that word into your transitions, like so. Transition of sequence: "This leads to..." becomes "This leads our journey to..." Transition of central message:

"This all comes down to..." becomes "The journey all comes down to..." Transition of continuation: "This continues until..." becomes "Our journey continues until..." etc. You're essentially taking your theme and attaching it to your transitions. Why do this? It reinforces your theme. It helps your audience remember your main message. It reminds your audience, during your speech, what your big idea is, all from adding a word or two to your existing transitions.

## DIRECT REQUESTS

Direct requests are persuasive. They are commanding. They give you control. And they work as transitions. Here are some examples: "Listen to this..." "Let me tell you..." "Guess what?" "Pay attention to this..." All of these direct request speech transitions are crisp, clear, and commanding. They get you attention and focus.

## I KNOW WHAT YOU'RE THINKING

Here are some examples: "Now I know what you're thinking..." "At this point you're probably wondering..." "I know you probably think..." Why are these so powerful? Not only are they smooth, engaging, and captivating speech transitions, but they connect you to your audience. If you can even come close to actually guessing what your audience is thinking at a given moment, you immediately get their attention. And if you don't? That's fine too. The transition is still an attention-grabber. And they'll instantly think what you mistakenly guessed they were already thinking, now that you popped the thought into their heads.

## FOMO TRANSITION

FOMO stands for "fear of missing out." And when you use this transition, you make your audience fear missing what you're about to say. Here are some examples: "You can't miss this..." "You'll regret it if you miss this next..." "You don't want to miss this big reveal..." Yes. Find a point in your speech where audience attention might be low. Insert an interesting, shocking piece of information. Insert a FOMO transition right at that point, before saying the interesting piece of information. This uses a FOMO transition right when you need it most.

## HUGE DISCOVERY

These transitions tell you audience that you have a huge discovery coming next. And they love hearing huge discoveries. Want to instantly regain audience attention? Want to transition into a big discovery? Use this transition. It does both. Here are some examples: "And then I discovered the most incredible secret..." "What I found out next was earth-shattering..." "I discovered something that blew my mind..." These become even more attention-grabbing with a method I call "transition stacking." But we'll talk about that later.

## UNFORTUNATE CATCH

Use this transition after describing something good, with no flaws presented. Use it to present the first flaw. "Unfortunately, there's a catch..." "It would work perfectly, except for..." "But there's one problem that breaks it..." It's a good way to regain the audience's attention. They'll all be thinking: "What's the flaw? Why doesn't it work?" And you will answer the question already in their minds.

## HIDDEN ANSWER

This one is highly effective at grabbing attention. Here's why it works: it teases a huge secret answer to a big question, which immediately builds curiosity. You have encountered similar strategies before. Never forget: curiosity commands attention. Make sure you state the question. Some examples: "And here's the answer to the question of..." "And the answer that nobody seems to know is..." "The correct answer is not what you'd think, it is really..." Questions create open loops. Open loops create curiosity. Curiosity creates a burning desire to discover the unknown. Hidden-answer transitions hint at upcoming loop-closers that satisfy curiosity.

### EXEMPLARY EXAMPLE

People learn through examples. And these transitions show them that a perfect example is coming up. Here are some examples of the exemplary example transition: "And a perfect example of this is..." "A perfect example of this exact phenomenon is..." "And this is expressed perfectly by..." Using words like "perfect" and "exact," show your audience that this example, in particular, is one they shouldn't miss.

---

KEY INSIGHT:

# Don't Speak Merely the Language of Theory. Accompany It with the Language of Example.

# Examples Make Facts Stick In the Mind By Emphasizing the Essence of What They Exemplify.

---

## HOW TO

Here are some examples: "Now, I'll teach you exactly how to..." "If you're wondering how to do it, here's how..." "Here's how you can do the exact same thing..." If your audience could choose only one part of your speech to listen to, it would probably be the one where you explain how to do something. Why? Because that provides them unique value. And when you use this transition, you indicate to them that you're giving them exactly what they want. Using words like "exactly" builds the impression that this is a bullet-proof, trustworthy, guaranteed process; that it is a precise solution to their specific problem.

## BIG SECRET

Here are some examples: "The hidden, little-known secret nobody else knows is that..." "The big secret about this is..." "The secret about what I just told you is that..." Why are these transitions so powerful? Let me remind you: they create open loops, open loops create curiosity, and curiosity creates instant attention.

## CURIOUS QUESTION

Curious questions create curiosity. Here are some examples: "What does this all mean?" "So, what's really going on here? "What's the real reason this is happening?" When you use questions like these, you create curiosity. Now, you're probably wondering: "Why do all of these transitions do the same thing?" Because a curious audience is an attentive one, and an attentive audience is the only kind of audience you can persuade. Using words like "really," and "real reason" imply that you're going straight to the truth and that it isn't what they heard before.

## BENEFIT TRANSITIONS

Your audience is always thinking "WIIFM." "Why should I listen? How will I benefit from this? How is this speaker helping me?" And with these transitions, you tell your audience what's in it for them. You answer those selfish questions. Here are some examples: "Now, you'll learn how to [insert benefit one], [insert benefit two], and [insert benefit three]." "What I'm going to tell you will help you [insert benefit]." "If you want to [insert benefit], here's how..." The moment you tell your audience what's in it for them is the moment you get their attention. And if it's been a long time since you've hit upon the WIIFM question, it's time to hit upon it again with this transition to renew attention. Think to yourself: "What do they truly want? What are they trying to achieve? What motivates them?" And then: "How does this relate to my speech?" Put those two things together, add this transition to the mix, and your audience's attention is yours.

## GUESS WHAT HAPPENED

Yes. More curiosity. Here's how you use this transition: "And guess what happened next?" "Try figuring out what happened next for a moment." "Will you even believe what happened next?" Simple. Elegant. Powerful.

## STAY WITH ME

This is another kind of direct command. Remember direct commands? They are persuasive and attention grabbing. These transitions sound like this: "Stay with me..." "Pay attention to this..." "Stick with me..." Use these to reinforce audience attention during difficult segments. What do I mean by difficult segments? Parts of your speech that are complex, technical in nature, or have a high cognitive load. It's during these moments when your audience decides to stop paying attention. But, if you include one of these transitions, you'll pull them along.

## INFORMATION SCENT TRANSITIONS

As a review: people forage for information like animals forage for food. And they use something called "information scent" to determine if they should pay attention. Remember, attention is a resource. So, information scent transitions do exactly what they sound like they do. They increase the information scent. Here's a step-by-step process: Figure out exactly what your audience wants to know above all. Precede that in your speech with an "information scent" transition. "I promise that you'll learn exactly how to [insert primary audience interest]." "You'll learn a simple step-by-step process to [insert primary audience interest]." "If you want to know how to [insert primary audience interest], I'm about to tell you." These increase information scent. They indicate incoming information. They grab attention.

## OPEN-LOOP TRANSITIONS

Open loops are a secret weapon of maintaining attention. These transitions have open-loops engineered directly into them. Here's a step-by-step process: Find an attention-grabbing secret to tease. Engineer that into existing transitions. For example: "In a few minutes, I'll teach you [insert tease], but first..." "You'll learn [insert tease], but before that..." "I'm going to show you [insert tease], right after we talk about..." Usually, the secrets are benefit-driven.

## RHETORICAL QUESTIONS

You know what they are. You don't know how you can turn any transition into one. So, here are some examples. Transition of sequence: "This leads to..." becomes "What does this all lead to?"

Transition to central message: "This all comes down to..." becomes "What does this all come down to?" Transition of continuation: "This continues until..." becomes "How far does this continue?" If you want to become more eloquent, use transitions. Want to become even more eloquent after that? Then turn your transitions into rhetorical questions.

## UNCERTAINTY

Secrecy sells. And uncertainty is accidental secrecy. So, engineer it into your transitions. Here are some examples: "And what we're all uncertain about is..." "What nobody understands yet is..." "The big, frustrating, unanswered question is..." Before the internet and the information age, people craved finding things that were certain. Now that we are inundated with information, people love uncertain things. So, if you use these transitions to tease uncertainty, you'll get more attention, you'll create intrigue, and you'll be more memorable.

**UNCERTAINTY INCREASES THE DEMAND FOR CERTAINTY**

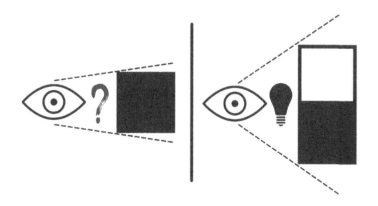

FIGURE 41: Black seems darker next to white, and white lighter next to black. Uncertainty, instigated correctly, can

increase the demand and the impulsive leap toward certainty – certainty in the form of agreeing with you.

## BEHIND THE SCENES

People love being insiders. People love knowing things that other people don't. People love feeling like they have exclusive information. And can you guess how behind the scenes transitions make people feel? Like insiders. Like they know information others don't. Like they have exclusive information. That's why these are so powerful. Here are some examples: "What happens behind the scenes is..." "As an insider, I'll tell you what nobody else knows..." "If you want the exclusive, behind-the-scenes look, here it is..."

### HOW TO EARN TRUST WHILE CAPTIVATING ATTENTION

SET OF POSSIBLE KNOWLEDGE

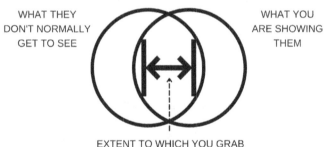

WHAT THEY DON'T NORMALLY GET TO SEE

WHAT YOU ARE SHOWING THEM

EXTENT TO WHICH YOU GRAB ATTENTION BY PULLING BACK THE CURTAIN

FIGURE 42: The overlap between what they don't normally get to see and what you are showing them is the extent to which you are grabbing attention by pulling back the veil.

## REFRESHER PHRASES

A lot of these previous transitions are refresher phrases. In fact, refresher phrases aren't a distinct set of transitions. Refresher phrases are transitions specifically designed to refresh an audience's attention span. Here's how they work: they tease information that is interesting, important, secretive, or valuable. They come before sentences containing that information. They subconsciously indicate to your audience that something important is coming. They front-load and shorten the transition, usually placing the transition on the left side of a colon and the sentence on the right. But, more importantly, here's why they work: when you say "Here's the secret:" (a refresher phrase), your audience is thinking "What's the secret? I love secrets. I better pay attention." When you say "Here's the solution:" your audience is thinking "I need the solution. This seems important. I'll listen up."

## DELAYED TRANSITIONS

We discussed these in passing, but I would like to share more about them. What do they do? They heighten pace. They heighten intensity. They shorten sentences. Delayed transitions are one-word transitions: "And..." "Now..." "But..." "Since..." They create the sensation of receiving more information in less time, which is true because they are shorter. And they maintain simplicity.

## THE TRUTH

This one is captivating. It will quickly grab audience attention. Why? Because people love truth, especially when it is handed to them and they don't have to search for it. Want to grab attention before making a statement? Want to inject confidence into that statement? Want your audience to see you as an honest, trustworthy speaker, and to take what you say as though an expert just told them the information? Then use this type of transition. "Now, the truth is..." "But the brutal truth is..." "Here's the truth..."

## HOW TO AVOID THE NINE SPEECH TRANSITION MISTAKES

These are the nine most common transition mistakes that undermine the very purpose of transition statements. Instead of keeping attention and smoothly transferring it from point to point, from the start of your speech to the end, transitions undermined by these mistakes will confuse the audience and weaken your hold on their attention.

## WRONG TRANSITION

This is the most common mistake you might make. In fact, I'm 100% positive that you've made this mistake at some point in the past. Here's what happened next: your audience got confused, you lost your train of thought, and your speech became unclear, blurry, and confusing. What is this big mistake? Applying the wrong transition. Applying a transition that doesn't match the relationship between the previous sentence and the next sentence. As you know, transitions are supposed to connect sentences (and other units of meaning). They tell your audience information about what you're going to say next. They are words spoken about the words you're going to speak next. The best transition to use (in fact, the only one to use), is the one that accurately connects sentence A and sentence B. For example, if sentence A and sentence B are describing two different things, the best transition to use is a difference transition, like "on the contrary." The wrong transition to use is anything other than a difference transition. Any transition that does not accurately represent the relationship between sentence A and B is the wrong transition. To help you prevent this mistake, I gave you more examples of transitions than you'll find anywhere else, broken down into more categories than you'll find anywhere else.

## TANGENTS

Tangents blur the clarity of your speaking. They confuse your audience. They muddy your message. Usually, you can tell when you're about to go on a tangent when you say a tangent transition: "This reminds me of a time..." "Ironically..." "A friend of mine once..." Now, here's the truth: tangents aren't all that bad. For informal, conversational speeches, one layer of tangents is okay. Why? Because it builds the speaker to audience connection and contributes to the relaxed atmosphere. However, two or more layers of tangents are not. In other words, if you are giving a relaxed, funny, personal speech, then one tangent is okay. But if you then launch into another tangent off of the previous tangent, that's bad. You have to first return to your linear speech. That's what "two layers of tangents" means. So be careful for this pattern: Tangent transition. Tangent. Another tangent transition. That pattern indicates two layers of tangents. This pattern is acceptable: Tangent transition. Tangent. "Back to what I was saying..." Main speech.

## MISSING TRANSITIONS

There's only one situation in which you shouldn't use transitions, which we will discuss shortly. Except for that one situation, you should always use transitions. Without transitions, your audience is wondering: "What does this sentence have to do with the last one?" "What is this person going to say next?" "How does this speech fit together?" Remember, you don't have to provide transitions between every single sentence or every single unit of meaning; just when it might not be clear what the relationship between the units of meaning is, when it is a major shift between very different units of meaning, or when people might get lost if they don't have a transition.

## REPETITIVE TRANSITIONS

Never repeat your transitions. Sure, you can use transitions of difference over and over. That's fine. But the problem arises when you use the same exact transition of difference over and over. Let's say you need to use three consecutive transitions of difference. Don't do it this way: "On the contrary... [sentence one]." "On the contrary... [sentence two]." "On the contrary... [sentence three]." Instead, do it this way: "On the contrary... [sentence one]." "As opposed to... [sentence two]." "Unlike... [sentence three]."

## MISCOUNT

Let's say you're listing out something in your speech. Maybe you're listing the steps of a process, a sequence of events, or your points. Here's what a miscount looks like: "First, you do..." "Second, you do..." "Next, you do..." "Third, you do..." There are four items in that list, but your list transition words don't show that. Why? Because instead of signposting the list items correctly, you accidentally replaced "third" with "next," and then made "fourth" into "third."

## REDUNDANT TRANSITIONS

What do these three examples of transitions have in common? "On the contrary, different than..." "Similarly, just like..." "Furthermore, additionally..." They are redundant. If you say "on the contrary," you don't need any other difference indicators. If you say "similarly," "just like" is redundant. If you say "furthermore," "additionally" is redundant. This is not the meaning of transition stacking, a strategy that can repeat transitions appropriately.

## TOO LONG

Transitions are important. Critical. But they shouldn't be running the show. Transitions are supposed to support your sentences, not the other way around. Any given sentence has a limited number of words in it before it stops making sense. Before it starts to be a run-on. Before it becomes confusing. Don't strain your sentences by using transitions that are way too long. For example, don't say "completely contrary and different to what we just talked about is..." Just say "on the contrary." That's much more easy, elegant, end efficient. Moving on to (an opposite) mistake.

**KEY INSIGHT:**

# Transitions Support the Key Parts of Your Message. They Should Draw Attention Toward What Comes After Them, Not Away From It.

# If They Distract From It, They Defeat Their Own Purpose.

## TOO SHORT

Transitions are too important. They have to be clear. You have to take the time to clearly put what you're about to say in context. Otherwise it makes less sense. So, while short transitions do have their place, an entire speech with short, unclear transitions is no good. As a general rule: transitions *within* the structural units of your speeches (sentence A to sentence B) can be short. Transitions between the structural unit (part one to part two, like problem to solution) need to be more defined and longer.

## UNCLEAR

Clever transitions help nobody. Choose clear over clever every chance you get. The best way to word your transitions (in fact, to word anything) is to say exactly what you mean, with the fewest number of words, with the simplest words possible, in a way that accurately connects your previous sentence to your next one (with regards to transitions).

## NINE ADVANCED SECRETS OF SPEECH TRANSITIONS

Did you know that you could stack transitions to instantly captivate an audience? Well, you can. And I'll show you how. These nine speech transition secrets are what set the pros apart from the amateurs. For example, the transitional body language technique. Even expert public speakers don't know that one. But you will. Let's dive right into it.

## TRANSITIONAL BODY LANGUAGE

It's simple: if you combine your transitions with transitional body language, they become twice as effective. Here some ways to do this:

for list transitions, list out the items on your fingers. For transitions of difference, hold your hands up in two fists, and move them away from each other. For transitions of similarity, bring your hands together. For transitions of continuation, take your hand and move it forward. For transitions of scale, hold your hands out wide. The big idea is that your body should send the same message as your words. Here's another cool way to use transitional body language: if you're giving a speech around three main points, deliver your first one from the left corner of the stage. Then, as you transition to your second point, move to the middle. Last, when you transition to your third, move to the right corner of the stage. In this way you mirror the structural transitions of your speech. Here's another example, to spur your imagination: for the problem-solution structure, you can sit for the problem portion and stand for the solution. Sitting, you seem like a cool professional diagnosing a problem with their expert, precise, penetrating, scalpel-like perception. Standing? An excited, passionate, visionary of a leader advocating for the best possible path forward. (Only sit if the context necessitates it).

### THE THREE-POINT STAGE-MOVEMENT TECHNIQUE

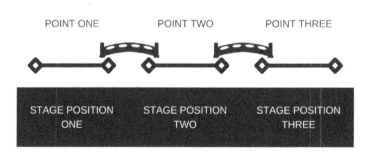

FIGURE 43: Move from stage position to stage position as you move from major point to major point.

## LACK OF TRANSITIONS

Every public speaking rule has exceptions. "Seriously?" you might be asking, slightly – or very – frustrated. Yes. And this is an exception to the "always use transitions" rule. Here are some examples of the extreme cases where you might not use transitions: When you want to build an extremely fast pace. When you want to build an extremely intense sequence. When you want to build an extremely snappy section.

That said, 99% of the time, you absolutely should use transitions. But if there's a segment in your speech where your most important rhetorical priority is intensity, then test the segment without transitions. Maybe it'll make it more intense.

## TRANSITION STACKING

What's better than an insanely captivating transition? Three insanely captivating transitions stacked together. Let's take a "big secret" transition. Not stacked: "The hidden, little–known secret nobody else knows is that..." Stacked: "You're about to learn the hidden, little-known secret few people know. You'll be among the first to know this. The big secret is..." When you stack transitions, you're amplifying their individual impacts. In this case, you amplify attention-grabbing effects: curiosity, suspense, and intrigue.

## TRANSITION WORDS

You're going to learn about transition words, phrases, and sentences. Specifically, you're going to learn when to use each. Use transition words to connect sentences when you want to heighten pace.

## TRANSITION PHRASES

Transition phrases are transitions that use multiple words. What advantages do they have over transition words? They are clearer. They more strongly indicate a transition. They make sure nobody misses the transition. But what disadvantages do they have? Well, they have one main disadvantage: they don't heighten pace as much as transition words do.

## TRANSITION SENTENCES

Transition sentences are transitions that take up full sentences, and if stacked, more sentences. Why are they good? Well, they're so incredibly clear that nobody misses them. In other words, they guarantee a smooth transition at a critical juncture. Time to put all this information together.

## THE TRANSITION MAP

Here's how to use transition words, phrases, and sentences: Use transition words when transitioning between sentences. Use transition phrases when transitioning between rhetorical segments. Use transition sentences when transitioning between structural shifts and paradigm shifts in the speech.

In other words, here's how transition words, phrases, and sentences match up to a speech structure: 1st main structural unit, transition with a sentence. 1st rhetorical sub-unit, transition with a phrase. Sentences within this: transition with single words. 2nd rhetorical sub-unit: transition with a phrase. Sentences within this: transition with single words. 2nd main structural unit: transition with a sentence. Repeat the pattern. This makes sure that the strength of your transition matches the size of your shift. Big structural shifts in a speech need big, obvious transitions (transition sentences). Smaller shifts between rhetorical sub-units need smaller transitions (transition phrases). The smallest shifts between individual sentences need the smallest transitions (transition words or short transition phrases).

### HOW TO SPEAK WITH PRISTINE ELOQUENCE

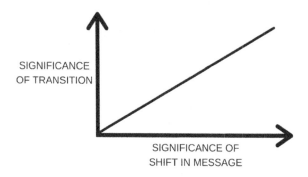

FIGURE 44: As the significance of the shift in your message rises, so too should the significance of your transition. This is the principle of the transition map.

## SPEECH STRUCTURE TRANSITIONS

Every structural shift should be accompanied by a big, obvious transition. This is exactly where transition stacking is most appropriate. For example, let's say you are using the problem-solution structure. When you're starting the problem unit of the structure, use a structural transition: a distinct transition that is significant and clearly marks the paradigm you are entering.

## TRICOLON TRANSITIONS

Want to be eloquent? Want your audiences to hang on your every word? Want your words to form a smooth flow? Then use tricolon transitions. Tricolons are phrases that incorporate lists of three. Here is an example of a regular "big-secret" transition: "The veiled secret is..." And now an example of a tricolon big–secret: "The veiled, hidden, little-known secret is..." It's a small change, but effective speaking is often accomplished by a series of small, subtle changes.

.............................Chapter Summary..............................

- While the opening formulas are designed to grab attention, transitions hold the role of keeping attention.
- Transitions answer the question "how is what I am about to say connected to what I just said?"
- Without transitions, you raise cognitive load. People need to figure out the connections between your points.
- Typically, raising cognitive load almost guarantees that you lose attention. People want to conserve cognitive energy.
- Transitions lower cognitive load, showing your audience how everything connects.
- Transitions smooth the flow of your speech, passing attention from point to point without any leakages.

**KEY INSIGHT:**

# Want to Intensify, Emphasize, or Lengthen a Part of Your Message? Turn a Lone Item Into a List of Three Thematically United Items.

## GRABBING, KEEPING, DIRECTING ATTENTION (PART TWO)

| 1 | Grabbing Attention |
|------|---------------------|
| 1.1 | Openings Are Make-or-Break Moments |
| 1.2 | Present a Personal Introduction After Grabbing Attention |
| 1.3 | Start with the Hook Before Your Personal Introduction |
| 1.4 | Recognize and Appeal to the Information-Foraging Dynamic |
| 1.5 | Maximize Information Scent Early on to Grab Attention |
| 1.6 | Speak with Crisp, Commanding Phrases to Drop Cognitive Load |
| 1.7 | Don't Stuff Your Sentences: One Idea Per Sentence at First |
| 1.8 | Begin with Fast Pace, High Energy, and Appropriate Intensity |
| 1.9 | Successfully Convey Value and Draw Interest in 15 Seconds |
| 1.10 | Master Openings: 20% of the Effort Produces 80% of the Results |
| 1.11 | Create Your Own Opening Formulas By Recombining the Steps |
| 1.12 | Shorten and Lengthen the Frameworks Like an Accordion |
| 1.13 | Use The Openings at Any Point to Regain and Strengthen Attention |
| 2 | Keeping Attention |
| 2.1 | "However, But, And, Resulting, So, etc." Exemplify Transitions |
| 2.2 | Transitions Carry Attention From Point to Point and Clarify Flow |
| 2.3 | Good Transitions Answer "How Does This Connect to That?" |
| 2.4 | Effective Transitions Both Clarify Meaning and Renew Interest |
| 2.5 | Introduce a Main Point with a Transition Revealing Its Significance |

| 2.6 | Wrong Transitions Don't Accurately Describe the Connection |
|------|-----------------------------------------------------------|
| 2.7 | Certain Transitions Signal a Tangent: Watch Out for Them |
| 2.8 | Generally, You Should Aim to Use Transitions |
| 2.9 | Repetitive Transitions Announce Themselves: Avoid Them |
| 2.10 | When Using List-Based Transitions, Watch Out for Miscounts |
| 2.11 | Redundant Transitions Are Unnecessary: Remove Them |
| 2.12 | Transitions That Are Too Long Begin to Blur Clarity, Losing Interest |
| 2.13 | Transitions That Are Too Short Fail to Indicate the Connection |
| 2.14 | Transitions That Are Unclear Often Raise Cognitive Load |
| 2.15 | Combine Major Transitions with Transitional Body Language |
| 2.16 | Missing Transitions Can, Used Correctly, Build Intense Rhythm |
| 2.17 | Transition Stacking Emphasizes a Shift, Renewing Interest |
| 2.18 | Single-Word Transitions Lower Cognitive Load Massively |
| 2.19 | Transition Phrases Are the "Standard" Length |
| 2.20 | Transition Sentences Transition in a Full Sentence |
| 2.21 | Use Single-Word Transitions Between Sentences |
| 2.22 | Use Transition-Phrases Between Paragraphs |
| 2.23 | Use Sentence-Transitions Between Major Shifts in the Message |
| 2.24 | Practice Mirroring the Speech Structure with a Transition Map |
| 2.25 | Tricolon Transitions Incorporate Eloquent Lists of Three |

206 | The Psychology of Communication

| 3 | Directing Attention |

Email Peter D. Andrei, the author of the Speak for Success collection and the President of Speak Truth Well LLC directly.

pandreibusiness@gmail.com

KEY INSIGHT:

# New Points Should Relate to the Idea That Came Before.

# But This Relation Is Not Always Obvious, Which Can Confuse the Audience.

# Clear Transitions Solve That Problem. They Keep People Onboard the Ship.

## YOU CAN STACK DIFFERENT TYPES OF TRANSITIONS TOGETHER FOR ADDED IMPACT

### BIG SECRET TRANSITION

And this brings us to our next point, which almost nobody I've ever spoken to knows.

### BENEFIT TRANSITION

And that's unfortunate, because this strategy reduces expenses by up to 20% in some cases.

### THE TRUTH TRANSITION

The brutal truth is that most other consultants have an incentive to hide this strategy. Not us.

## YOU CAN STACK DIFFERENT HOOK STRUCTURES TOGETHER FOR ADDED IMPACT

### MOMENT, FUTURE, DECISION

Right now, our country is falling apart.
But we can fix it. The choice is ours.

### QUESTION, PROMISE, PREVIEW

You may be wondering, "Is there still hope?"
There is. But the solution isn't easy.

### BENEFIT, BENEFIT, BENEFIT, DELAY

It can unite us, strengthen our culture, and
revive our economy. In a minute, I'll share it...

**Claim These Free Resources that Will Help You Unleash the Power of Your Words and Speak with Confidence. Visit <u>www.speakforsuccesshub.com/toolkit</u> for Access.**

### 18 Free PDF Resources

*12 Iron Rules for Captivating Story, 21 Speeches that Changed the World, 341-Point Influence Checklist, 143 Persuasive Cognitive Biases, 17 Ways to Think On Your Feet, 18 Lies About Speaking Well, 137 Deadly Logical Fallacies, 12 Iron Rules For Captivating Slides, 371 Words that Persuade, 63 Truths of Speaking Well, 27 Laws of Empathy, 21 Secrets of Legendary Speeches, 19 Scripts that Persuade, 12 Iron Rules For Captivating Speech, 33 Laws of Charisma, 11 Influence Formulas, 219-Point Speech-Writing Checklist, 21 Eloquence Formulas*

**Claim These Free Resources that Will Help You Unleash the Power of Your Words and Speak with Confidence. Visit www.speakforsuccesshub.com/toolkit for Access.**

**30 Free Video Lessons**

We'll send you one free video lesson every day for 30 days, written and recorded by Peter D. Andrei. Days 1-10 cover authenticity, the prerequisite to confidence and persuasive power. Days 11-20 cover building self-belief and defeating communication anxiety. Days 21-30 cover how to speak with impact and influence, ensuring your words change minds instead of falling flat. Authenticity, self-belief, and impact – this course helps you master three components of confidence, turning even the most high-stakes presentations from obstacles into opportunities.

**Claim These Free Resources that Will Help You Unleash
the Power of Your Words and Speak with Confidence. Visit
<u>www.speakforsuccesshub.com/toolkit</u> for Access.**

**2 Free Workbooks**

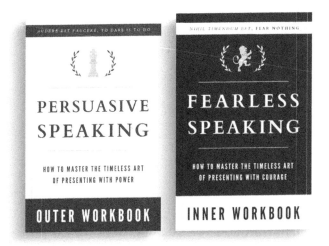

We'll send you two free workbooks, including long-lost excerpts by
Dale Carnegie, the mega-bestselling author of *How to Win Friends
and Influence People* (5,000,000 copies sold). *Fearless Speaking*
guides you in the proven principles of mastering your inner game as a
speaker. *Persuasive Speaking* guides you in the time-tested tactics of
mastering your outer game by maximizing the power of your words.
All of these resources complement the Speak for Success collection.

**SPEAK FOR SUCCESS COLLECTION BOOK**

# XIV

**THE PSYCHOLOGY OF COMMUNICATION CHAPTER**

# IV

# THE ENDING:
## Directing Attention

## HOW TO END COMMUNICATION

T HESE PROVEN ENDINGS FOR YOUR persuasive communication will end strong, ensure that the audience remembers your speech, and wrap up in a way that impacts people and directs attention toward a meaningful purpose.

## THE BASICS OF COMMUNICATION ENDINGS

If you don't understand the basics of how to end your communication, know this: it will be much more difficult to persuade people and to end a speech (or any communication) with power. Why is that? Because these basics characterize all effective communication conclusions. Without them, no conclusion can effectuate long-lasting change in the audience.

### HOW TO MASTER THE ART OF THE CONCLUSION

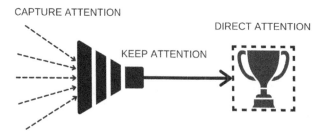

FIGURE 45: The conclusion is designed to take all of the attentional momentum you have cultivated, and focus it like a laser on a worthy goal.

## THE GOALS OF CONCLUSIONS

Persuasive communication conclusions work if these following conditions are met: You have made your message memorable. You have provided a "hard" call to action. You have provided a "soft" call to action. You have provided future triggers. You have provided the ingredients for future confirmation bias. You have reminded the audience of benefits. You have made action appear easy. You have struck while the iron was hot. You have subtly represented your detachment to outcome. You have simplified to your core message. If your communication endings can do these ten things, then you have succeeded.

## MEMORABLE

You can make your message memorable by repeating your core points in a brief summary and by delivering one particularly eloquent and memorable "tagline" that summarizes your message in one sentence.

### CREATE A SENTENTIA OR "TAGLINE" STATEMENT

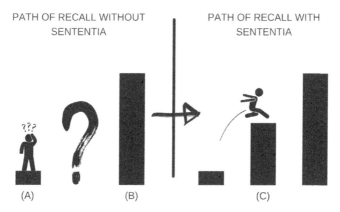

PATH OF RECALL WITHOUT SENTENTIA

PATH OF RECALL WITH SENTENTIA

(A)                    (B)                    (C)

FIGURE 46: Going from no recall (A) to full recall (B) is difficult without a stepping stone. A sententia or tagline statement allows people to make the leap from no recall to full recall with greater ease (C).

## MEMORABILITY IS PERSUASION: THE AVAILABILITY BIAS

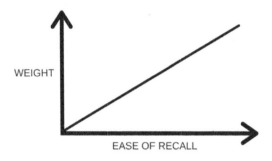

FIGURE 47: The more easily recalled your message is, the greater weight people afford to it. This is known as the availability bias.

## CALL TO ACTION

You must include a call to action in the end of your speech, even if it is an informational speech. How? Here's an example of a call to action that works for an informational speech: "After learning all about voter suppression throughout the United States, I urge you to remember not to take your right to vote for granted." This is called a "soft" call to action. Persuasive speeches tend to demand a "hard" call to action: "take action X," where X is often buying something, voting for someone, or exchanging some resource for a desired outcome by taking some action. But informational speeches and inspirational speeches tend to demand a soft call to action: thinking a certain way, for example.

## SOFT AND HARD CALL TO ACTION

The best closings for persuasive communication include both hard and soft calls to action. A hard call to action is the main goal: "vote for candidate X," for example. But a soft call to action can be a plan B for the audience members who aren't ready to follow the hard call to action.

**GUARANTEEING PERSUASIVE SUCCESS 100% OF THE TIME**

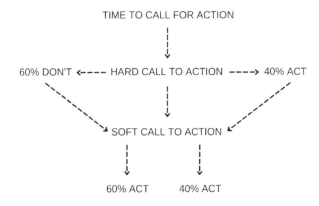

FIGURE 48: While not everyone may act on your hard, tangible call to action, almost everyone will act on your soft call to action. Present both.

## FUTURE TRIGGERS

Want your audience to remember your hard or soft call to action? Want your core message to instantly pop into their heads long into the future? Here's how you can do that: use triggers. Anchor your message to a very common situation that involves the VAKOG senses. When it happens, that anchor will trigger a powerful recollection of your message.

## HOW TO TRIGGER RECALL OF YOUR MESSAGE

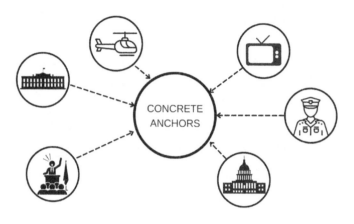

FIGURE 49: Anchor your message to concrete, visual experiences that will reoccur over and over again. This will prompt repeated recall of your message.

## FUTURE CONFIRMATION BIAS

Simply plant the seeds in the minds of your audience members for future confirmation bias. Confirmation bias is the tendency to interpret new evidence as confirmation of existing beliefs or theories. For example, if your message is "Democratic politicians want to silence us!" then you can anchor this not only to a trigger, but to a trigger that appeals to confirmation bias: "And every time you see them say [insert a common and very benign saying of Democratic politicians], I want you to see that as what it really is – them trying to silence the conservative movement." This way, every time a Democrat does say that, it will trigger a recollection of this particular speaker's message, and a trigger that plays into confirmation bias. In other words, the audience will interpret this new information as evidence of their currently held belief, which the speaker planted in their minds (that Democrats want to silence conservatives).

## HOW TO TRIGGER AGREEMENT WITH YOUR MESSAGE

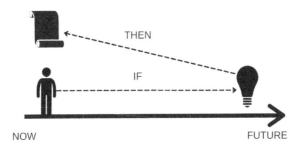

FIGURE 50: In the moment of your speech, present a trigger in the following format: "if (in the future) X happens, then remember Y (my message)."

## BENEFITS

I'll say it for the fifth or sixth time in this book: benefits sell. And what better time to drop benefits on your audience members than the conclusion of your speech? And if you tie your benefits to your call to action, it increases perceived marginal gain of following your action, hopefully pushing it beyond perceived marginal loss, and thereby creating action. So tie benefits to your call to action in a format like this, for example: "So if you (or we) want [insert benefit one], [insert benefit two], and [insert benefit three], what you (or we) have to do is [insert call to action]." And while this increase perceived marginal benefit, the next technique decreases perceived marginal cost, thereby further balancing that one critical equation in your favor.

**"WHAT DO I GAIN IF I DO WHAT YOU WANT ME TO DO?"**

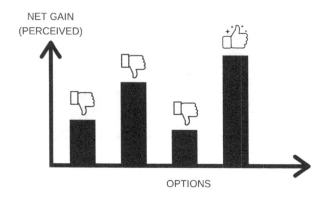

FIGURE 51: This visualizes the fundamental algorithm people perform that determines what action they will take.

## EASE

After benefits, throw in ease. In other words, make taking your desired action appear much easier. Use phrases like these: "quick," "easy," "simple," "step-by-step," and minimizing phrases like: "*only a small amount of* [insert resource cost, whether money or time].

**KEY INSIGHT:**

# On Some Level of Our Being, We Don't Just Want To Get Good Things; We Want to Get Them As Easily as Possible.

## BALANCING THE ENERGY IN, ENERGY OUT EQUATION

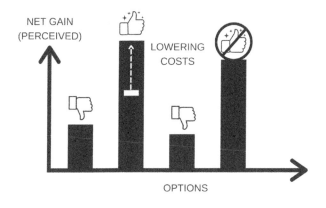

FIGURE 52: Net gain is gain minus costs. Lowering costs therefore raises net gain.

## "HOT IRON"

There will be a time when your audience, more than any other time in your speech, is in a mental state most conducive to taking your desired action. If you have a good idea of when this will be, why not conclude right then and there, and strike while the iron is hot? Mental states are not permanent. So, if you know that your audience is in a conducive mood at a particular point in time, that's when you should strike with the call to action.

## DON'T MAKE THIS CRUCIAL PERSUASIVE MISTAKE

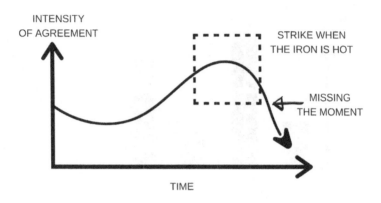

FIGURE 53: Present your conclusive sentiments when the iron is hot; when the intensity of the agreement is highest. Don't miss the moment by striking when the iron cooled.

## DETACHMENT

This one is interesting, and serves to raise your personal dignity, maintain a positive relationship with your audience members, and decrease pressure. All this means is expressing to your audience that you are grateful for the chance to speak with them no matter what they decide to do. For example: "I'm grateful that you gave me the chance to speak to you today. I really hope you learned a lot and are better equipped to make this decision. That's what really matters to me here." Note that you shouldn't say them taking the action doesn't matter, because that is obviously not true (if it didn't matter you wouldn't be speaking to them about it). All you're saying is that you have a more benevolent motive that has already been fulfilled, no matter what the audience member decides to do. Hopefully this is actually true, and not just a rhetorical technique, because detachment from outcome paradoxically produces better outcomes in the world by creating a better mindset which produces better actions that create those outcomes.

## SIMPLIFY

Make it simple. No matter what you choose to do for your closing, at the very least include a one sentence summary of your main message. If you can't say it in one sentence, you can't say it in an entire speech.

## TEN PROVEN STRATEGIES FOR ENDING COMMUNICATION WITH POWER

Now that we went over the basics of how to end persuasive communication, we're going to go over some proven strategies for how to end your persuasive communication with efficacy and style. These ten proven strategies are going to instantly take the confusion and anxiety out of ending your communication, and give you easy and reliable guidelines to follow that are specifically designed to end with impact, directing the attention you grabbed and kept to a useful end goal.

## MICRO STRUCTURE REPETITION

Take your top-level structure, break down each step into one sentence, and deliver these sentences at the end of your speech in a summary of your overall structure. In other words, shorten your structure to the point that each step is one sentence, and then deliver that as the ending of your speech.

## UNSCRIPTED PASSION

This was one of my favorite strategies. By the end of my competitive debate rounds (each one was one hour long, and there were five or six rounds per competition), I was not in the mood to write down my main ideas in the one-minute prep for closing statements, meticulously plan it all out, and deliver according to a prepared structure. I just cleared my head in that one minute, and let the passionate words flow out of me uninhibited when the time came. And I found that this was much better, in some cases, than going according to a planned structure. I always planned my openings, but by the end of the round, I was so warmed-up that it was no problem winging it, and not only was it just not a problem, it was actually the best strategy.

## HOPE

If you're talking about a problem, and you want people to solve it, then ending on hope is a very powerful strategy. Why? Because if a problem is hopeless, why even *try* to solve it? By ending on hope, you increase the chance that your audience will take an action to solve a problem, because they now believe the problem is actually solvable. Don't fall into the doom-and-gloom trap: fear and loss are powerful motivators, but they have to be coupled with a true hope that the fear and loss can be prevented. If not? People won't do anything.

## REVIEW OUTCOME

This one is simple: all you have to do is review the outcome of your speech. It's good for casual informational speeches. "Today, you learned exactly how to do [insert action]. You learned how to avoid beginner mistakes, like [insert beginner mistakes]. And you learned how you can use [insert action] to get [insert benefits]."

## REMEMBER THIS

This one is easy: it uses direct requests, and is simple to formulate. All you have to do is this: identify the one idea you want your audience to remember, and tell them you want them to remember it. "But the crucial truth about [insert subject] that any informed citizen must remember, and that I want you to remember, is [insert what you want them to remember]."

## MORAL

This one depends on your speech: are you speaking about a set of themes? Perhaps speaking in terms of a narrative or chronology? Are you telling stories or reciting history? If so, do this: identify the one moral lesson about life that can be drawn from your stories, and introduce it by specifically enumerating it in your closing: "So what can we learn from this story? What does it mean? Here's the moral: [insert moral]."

## MATTER OF FACT

This one is fun: all you have to do is introduce a summary, review, central moral, or *anything* you want your audience to remember, with the assertive "matter-of-fact" phrases: "The fact of the matter is that…" "The fact is that…" "The truth about this is…"

## EMPOWERMENT

This one is perhaps the best: close your speech by empowering your audience. Leave them with whatever gift your speech gave them, plus some inspiration that they can use the gift, and have the personal power to take positive action.

## FORK IN THE ROAD

This one is captivating: present two possible paths forward, and the position your audience is in right now as that moment when a challenging fork in the road is ahead. It adds a sense of serious sentiment to the moment. It makes them think "This is real. We have to make a choice. The time to decide who we are going to be is now."

## SUMMARY

This is a standard one: just summarize your speech; the main takeaways, the big ideas, some evidence, and what it means for your audience. Take the most important sentence from each section of your speech, reword it, and repeat it at the end.

## EASY, STEP–BY–STEP ENDING FORMULAS

These ten easy, step-by-step ending formulas are yet another set of persuasive templates and patterns that you can simply fill in with your specific content. Not only do these make you infinitely more persuasive and compelling, but they also give you the benefit of ease: instead of confusion, you have a clear set of choices to choose from and simply fill in. This should reduce your anxiety about your presentation, writing, or speech. Let's get right into it. This chapter contains the last of the proven formulas for attention-grabbing communication, and will complete your toolbox of powerful speaking patterns.

## BENEFITS, EASE, CERTAINTY, SOFT CALL TO ACTION, HARD CALL TO ACTION

Benefits: "We will [insert benefit one], [insert benefit two], and [insert benefit three]." Ease: "We will do it with a process that only costs [insert dollar amount if applicable] and takes only [insert time commitment] to implement." Certainty: "This process is proven, tested, and guaranteed to get us [insert benefits] for just [insert resources necessary]." Soft call to action: "My work here will be complete if you recognize this as the immense opportunity that it is." Hard call to action: "But it's up to you to seize it by [insert first step]."

## HOPE, TOGETHERNESS, EMPOWERMENT, OUTCOME

Hope: "The future can be better: [insert how]." Togetherness: "Together, we can create a future that [insert positive characteristics]. Divided, we are resigned to a future that [insert negative characteristics]." Empowerment: "But I know we can come together and create incredible outcomes for everyone. We've done this before: [insert example one], [insert example two], and [insert example three]." Outcome: "And if we do it again, we can [insert positive vision of the future]."

## REVIEW OUTCOME, SUMMARY, REMEMBER THIS, SENTENTIA, TRIGGERS, CONFIRMATION BIAS

Review outcome: "If we take [insert action], we can [insert outcome]." Summary: "[insert sub-point one], [insert sub-point two], and [insert sub-point three]." Remember this: "I want you to remember [insert core message." Sententia (a rhetorically charged sentence summarizing the preceding material): "I want you to remember [insert sententia]." Triggers: "Every time you see [insert situation one], [insert situation two], and [insert situation three], I want you to remember what it really is." Confirmation bias: "I want you to remember that it is an example of [insert what it is an example of]."

## WE KNOW, WE KNOW, WE KNOW, QUESTION

We know: "We know that [insert agreed-upon fact]." We know: "We know that [insert second agreed-upon fact]." We know: "We know that [insert third agree-upon fact]." Question: "But what we don't know is this: will we [insert action] to create [insert positive outcome]?"

## BEFORE, AFTER, MEANS, FUTURE

Before: "When I first started speaking, you were [insert characteristics of insufficiency]." After: "Now, you are [insert characteristics of sufficiency]." Means: "This is because you are equipped with the knowledge of [insert subject]." Future: "This knowledge will allow you to [insert benefit one], [insert benefit two], and [insert benefit three]."

## REVIEW, USE, SOFT CALL TO ACTION

Review: "Today, you learned [insert subject]." Use: "I want you to rely on this knowledge every time [insert situation] happens." Soft call to action: "I want you to feel [insert positive emotions], knowing that what you learned about [insert subject] will equip you to succeed every time [insert situation] happens."

## NOT THIS, BUT THAT, INTENSIFYING REPETITION

Not this: "[insert situation] is not [insert archetypal situation]..." But that: "...but [insert other archetypal situation]." Intensifying repetition: "not [insert another more intense archetypal situation], but [another more intense archetypal situation]. Not [insert another even more intense archetypal situation], but [another more intense archetypal situation]." (By archetypal situation, I mean a common situation that reoccurs throughout history in the abstract. For example: "a situation of the strong oppressing the weak.")

## TRIGGER, CONFIRMATION BIAS, NOT THIS, BUT THAT

Trigger: "I want you to keep what I told you in mind every time you see [insert common occurrence]." Confirmation bias: "I want you to remember that [insert common occurrence] is an example of [insert your main point]." Not this: "I want you to remember that it is not a [insert archetypal situation]." But that: "I want you to remember that it is, in truth, a [insert the archetypal situation you said something is]."

## WHAT'S DONE, WHAT'S NEXT

What's done: "We've come a long way. We have [insert example one], [insert example two], and [insert example three]." What's next: "But there's much more that must still be done. We must [insert goal one], [insert goal two], and [insert goal three], by [insert means], because [insert reasons]."

## MAIN POINT, EVIDENCE, LOGIC, EMOTION

Main point: "The truth is that [insert your main point]." Evidence: "And we know this is true because [insert evidence]." Logic: "[insert evidence] means [insert main point] because [logical connections between evidence and claim]." Emotion: "[insert emotional agitators]."

...............................Chapter Summary...............................

- If you have grabbed and kept attention for a long time, directing it to a purpose or focal point is easier.
- There is a form of attentional momentum: the more you control attention, the more likely you are to control it.
- Some ending strategies simply call for presenting a particular meaning or sub-message.
- Other ending strategies are full-fledged long-form step-by-step formulas for you to fill in.
- As with opening strategies, you can stack ending strategies to form a more comprehensive and compelling finish.

- Grab attention, keep attention, and direct attention. This is the task of an effective communicator.

**KEY INSIGHT:**

# We Are Wired to Feel Deep Compassion Toward People, Not Abstractions.

# We Need Stories. We Use Stories to Organize Our Minds. No Story, No Meaning. No Meaning, No Impact.

## GRABBING, KEEPING, DIRECTING ATTENTION (PART THREE)

| 1 | Grabbing Attention |
|------|---------------------------------------------------------------------|
| 1.1 | Openings Are Make-or-Break Moments |
| 1.2 | Present a Personal Introduction After Grabbing Attention |
| 1.3 | Start with the Hook Before Your Personal Introduction |
| 1.4 | Recognize and Appeal to the Information-Foraging Dynamic |
| 1.5 | Maximize Information Scent Early on to Grab Attention |
| 1.6 | Speak with Crisp, Commanding Phrases to Drop Cognitive Load |
| 1.7 | Don't Stuff Your Sentences: One Idea Per Sentence at First |
| 1.8 | Begin with Fast Pace, High Energy, and Appropriate Intensity |
| 1.9 | Successfully Convey Value and Draw Interest in 15 Seconds |
| 1.10 | Master Openings: 20% of the Effort Produces 80% of the Results |
| 1.11 | Create Your Own Opening Formulas By Recombining the Steps |
| 1.12 | Shorten and Lengthen the Frameworks Like an Accordion |
| 1.13 | Use The Openings at Any Point to Regain and Strengthen Attention |
| 2 | Keeping Attention |
| 2.1 | "However, But, And, Resulting, So, etc." Exemplify Transitions |
| 2.2 | Transitions Carry Attention From Point to Point and Clarify Flow |
| 2.3 | Good Transitions Answer "How Does This Connect to That?" |
| 2.4 | Effective Transitions Both Clarify Meaning and Renew Interest |
| 2.5 | Introduce a Main Point with a Transition Revealing Its Significance |

| 2.6 | Wrong Transitions Don't Accurately Describe the Connection |
| 2.7 | Certain Transitions Signal a Tangent: Watch Out for Them |
| 2.8 | Generally, You Should Aim to Use Transitions |
| 2.9 | Repetitive Transitions Announce Themselves: Avoid Them |
| 2.10 | When Using List-Based Transitions, Watch Out for Miscounts |
| 2.11 | Redundant Transitions Are Unnecessary: Remove Them |
| 2.12 | Transitions That Are Too Long Begin to Blur Clarity, Losing Interest |
| 2.13 | Transitions That Are Too Short Fail to Indicate the Connection |
| 2.14 | Transitions That Are Unclear Often Raise Cognitive Load |
| 2.15 | Combine Major Transitions with Transitional Body Language |
| 2.16 | Missing Transitions Can, Used Correctly, Build Intense Rhythm |
| 2.17 | Transition Stacking Emphasizes a Shift, Renewing Interest |
| 2.18 | Single-Word Transitions Lower Cognitive Load Massively |
| 2.19 | Transition Phrases Are the "Standard" Length |
| 2.20 | Transition Sentences Transition in a Full Sentence |
| 2.21 | Use Single-Word Transitions Between Sentences |
| 2.22 | Use Transition-Phrases Between Paragraphs |
| 2.23 | Use Sentence-Transitions Between Major Shifts in the Message |
| 2.24 | Practice Mirroring the Speech Structure with a Transition Map |
| 2.25 | Tricolon Transitions Incorporate Eloquent Lists of Three |

| 3 | Directing Attention |
|---|---|
| 3.1 | Your Entire Message Builds Up to Your Conclusion |
| 3.2 | The Goal of Your Conclusion is to Empower Memory and Action |
| 3.3 | Your Conclusion Must Ensure Your Audience Recalls the Message |
| 3.4 | Your Conclusion Must Call them to Action |
| 3.5 | Soft Calls to Action Call for a Shift in Thinking or Approach |
| 3.6 | Hard Calls to Action Call for a Tangible Action: Use Both |
| 3.7 | Future Triggers Link Your Message to Events Triggering Memory |
| 3.8 | Future Confirmation Bias Empower Future Reconfirmation |
| 3.9 | Presenting Benefits in the Conclusion Increases Action |
| 3.10 | Presenting Ease in the Conclusion Increases Action |
| 3.11 | Strike While the Iron is Hot, Not After it Cooled Back Down |
| 3.12 | Present Your Detachment from the Outcome |
| 3.13 | Summarize the Message in the Conclusion |

**Email Peter D. Andrei, the author of the Speak for Success collection and the President of Speak Truth Well LLC directly.**

**pandreibusiness@gmail.com**

## SOMETHING WAS MISSING. THIS IS IT.

D ECEMBER OF 2021, I COMPLETED the new editions of the 15 books in the Speak for Success collection, after months of work, and many 16-hour-long writing marathons. The collection is over 1,000,000 words long and includes over 1,700 handcrafted diagrams. It is *the* complete communication encyclopedia. But instead of feeling relieved and excited, I felt uneasy and anxious. Why? Well, I know now. After writing over 1,000,000 words on communication across 15 books, it slowly dawned on me that I had missed the most important set of ideas about good communication. What does it *really* mean to be a good speaker? This is my answer.

### THERE ARE THREE DIMENSIONS OF SUCCESS

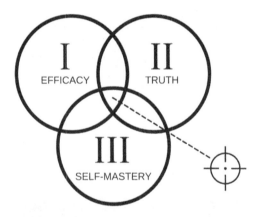

FIGURE I: A good speaker is not only rhetorically effective. They speak the truth, and they are students of self-mastery who experience peace, calm, and deep equanimity as they speak. These three domains are mutually reinforcing.

I realized I left out much about truth and self-mastery, focusing instead on the first domain. On page 33, the practical guide is devoted to domain I. On page 42, the ethical guide is devoted to domain II. We will shortly turn to domain III with an internal guide.

## WHAT A GOOD SPEAKER LOOKS LIKE

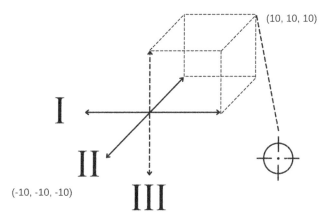

FIGURE II: We can conceptualize the three domains of success as an (X, Y, Z) coordinate plane, with each axis extending between -10 and 10. Your job is to become a (10, 10, 10). A (-10, 10, 10) speaks the truth and has attained self-mastery, but is deeply ineffective. A (10, -10, 10), speaks brilliantly and is at peace, but is somehow severely misleading others. A (10, 10, -10), speaks the truth well, but lives in an extremely negative inner state.

## THE THREE AXES VIEWED DIFFERENTLY

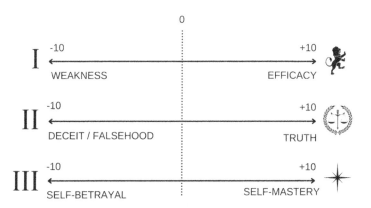

FIGURE III: We can also untangle the dimensions of improvement from representation as a coordinate plane, and instead lay them out flat, as spectrums of progress. A

(+10, -10, -10) is a true monster, eloquent but evil. A (10, 10, 10) is a Martin Luther King. A more realistic example is (4, -3, 0): This person is moderately persuasive, bends truth a little too much for comfort (but not horribly), and is mildly anxious about speaking but far from falling apart. Every speaker exists at some point along these axes.

## THE EXTERNAL MASTERY PROCESS IS INTERNAL TOO

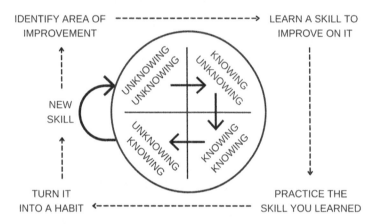

FIGURE IV: The same process presented earlier as a way to achieve rhetorical mastery will also help you achieve self-mastery. Just replace the word "skill" with "thought" or "thought-pattern," and the same cyclical method works.

## THE THREE AXES, IN DIFFERENT WORDS

| Domain One | Domain Two | Domain Three |
| --- | --- | --- |
| Efficacy | Truth | Self-Mastery |
| Rhetoric | Research | Inner-Peace |
| Master of Words | Seeker of Truth | Captain of Your Soul |
| Aristotle's "Pathos" | Aristotle's "Logos" | Aristotle's "Ethos" |
| Impact | Insight | Integrity |
| Presence of Power | Proper Perspective | Power of Presence |
| Inter-Subjective | Objective | Subjective |
| Competency | Credibility | Character |
| External-Internal | External | Internal |
| Verbal Mastery | Subject Mastery | Mental Mastery |
| Behavioral | Cognitive | Emotional |

## THE POWER OF LANGUAGE

Language has generative power. This is why many creation stories include language as a primordial agent playing a crucial role in crafting reality. "In the beginning was the Word, and the Word was with God (John 1:1)."

Every problem we face has a story written about its future, whether explicit or implicit, conscious or subconscious. Generative language can rewrite a story that leads downward, turning it into one that aims us toward heaven, and then it can inspire us to realize this story. It can remove the cloud of ignorance from noble possibilities.

And this is good. You can orient your own future upward. That's certainly good for you. You can orient the future upward for yourself and for your family. That's better. And for your friends. That's better. And for your organization, your community, your city, and your country. That's better still. And for your enemies, and for people yet unborn; for all people, at all times, from now until the end of time.

And it doesn't get better than that.

Sound daunting? It is. It is the burden of human life. It is also the mechanism of moral progress. But start wherever you can, wherever you are. Start by acing your upcoming presentation.

But above all, remember this: all progress begins with truth.

Convey truth beautifully. And know thyself, so you can guard against your own proclivity for malevolence, and so you can strive toward self-mastery. Without self-mastery, it's hard, if not nearly impossible, to do the first part; to convey truth beautifully.

Truth, so you do good, not bad; impact, so people believe you; and self-mastery, as an essential precondition for truth and impact. Imagine what the world would be like if everyone were a triple-ten on our three axes. Imagine what good, what beauty, what bliss would define our existence. Imagine what good, what beauty, what bliss *could* define our existence, here and now.

It's up to you.

# THE INNER GAME OF SPEAKING

R EFER BACK TO THIS INTERNAL GUIDE as needed. These humble suggestions have helped me deliver high-stakes speeches with inner peace, calm, and equanimity. They are foundational, and the most important words I ever put to paper. I hope these ideas help you as much as they helped me.

MASTER BOTH GAMES. Seek to master the outer game, but also the inner game. The self-mastery game comes before the word-mastery game, and even the world-mastery game. In fact, if you treat *any* game as a way to further your self-mastery, setting this as your "game above all games," you can never lose.

ADOPT THREE FOUNDATIONS. Humility: "The other people here probably know something I don't. They could probably teach me something. I could be overlooking something. I could be wrong. They have something to contribute" Passion: "Conveying truth accurately and convincingly is one of the most important things I'll ever do." Objectivity: "If I'm wrong, I change course. I am open to reason. I want to *be* right; I don't just want to seem right or convince others I am."

STRIVE FOR THESE SUPERLATIVES. Be the kindest, most compassionate, most honest, most attentive, most well-researched, and most confident in the room. Be the one who cares most, who most seeks to uplift others, who is most prepared, and who is most thoughtful about the reason and logic and evidence behind the claims.

START BY CULTIVATING THE HIGHEST VIRTUES IN YOURSELF: love for your audience, love for truth, humility, a deep and abiding desire to make the world a better place, the desire to both be heard and to hear, and the desire to both teach and learn. You will find peace, purpose, clarity, confidence, and persuasive power.

START BY AVOIDING THESE TEMPTING MOTIVES. Avoid the desire to "outsmart" people, to overwhelm and dominate with your rhetorical strength, to embarrass your detractors, to win on the basis of cleverness alone, and to use words to attain power for its own sake. Don't set personal victory as your goal. Strive to achieve a victory for truth. And if you discover you are wrong, change course.

LISTEN TO YOURSELF TALK. (Peterson, 2018). See if what you are saying makes you feel stronger, physically, or weaker. If it makes you feel weaker, stop saying it. Reformulate your speech until you feel the ground under you solidifying.

SPEAK FROM A PLACE OF LOVE. It beats speaking from a desire to dominate. Our motivation and purpose in persuasion must be love. It's ethical *and* effective.

LOVE YOUR ENEMIES (OR HAVE NONE). If people stand against you, do not inflame the situation with resentment or anger. It does no good, least of all for you.

AVOID THESE CORRUPTING EMOTIONS: resistance, resentment, and anger. Against them, set acceptance, forgiveness, and love for all, even your enemies.

PLACE YOUR ATTENTION HERE, NOW. Be where you are. Attend to the moment. Forget the past. Forget the future. Nothing is more important than this.

FOCUS ON YOURSELF, BUT NOW. Speaking gurus will tell you to focus solely on your audience. Yes, that works. But so does focusing on yourself, as long as you focus on yourself *now*. Let this focus root you in the present. Don't pursue a mental commentary on what you see. Instead, just watch. Here. Now. No judgment.

ACCEPT YOUR FEAR. Everyone fears something. If you fear speaking, don't fear your fear of speaking too. Don't reprimand yourself for it. Accept it. Embrace it, even. Courage isn't action without fear. Courage is action despite fear.

STARE DOWN YOUR FEAR. To diminish your fear, stare at the object of your fear (and the fear itself), the way a boxer faces off with his opponent before the fight. Hold it in your mind, signaling to your own psyche that you can face your fear.

CHIP AWAY AT YOUR FEAR. The path out of fear is to take small, voluntary steps toward what you fear. Gradual exposure dissolves fear as rain carves stone.

LET THE OUTER SHAPE THE INNER. Your thoughts impact your actions. But your actions also impact your thoughts. To control fear, seek to manage its outward manifestations, and your calm exterior will shape your interior accordingly.

KNOW THAT EGO IS THE ENEMY. Ego is a black storm cloud blocking the warm sunlight of your true self. Ego is the creation of a false self that masquerades as your true self and demands gratification (which often manifests as the destruction of something good). The allure of arrogance is the siren-song of every good speaker. With it comes pride and the pursuit of power; a placing of the outer game before the inner. Don't fall for the empty promises of ego-gratification. Humility is power.

DON'T IDENTIFY WITH YOUR POSITIONS. Don't turn your positions into your psychological possessions. Don't imbue them with a sense of self.

NOTICE TOXIC AVATARS. When person A speaks to person B, they often craft a false idea, a false avatar, of both themselves and their interlocuter: A1 and B1. So does person B: B2 and A2. The resulting communication is a dance of false avatars; A1, B1, B2, and A2 communicate, but not person A and B. A false idea of one's self speaks to a false idea of someone else, who then does the same. This may be why George Bernard Shaw said "the greatest problem in communication is the illusion that it has been accomplished." How do you avoid this dance of false avatars? This conversation between concepts but not people? Be present. Don't prematurely judge. Let go of your *sense* of self, for just a moment, so your real self can shine forth.

MINE THE RICHES OF YOUR MIND. Look for what you need within yourself; your strengths and virtues. But also acknowledge and make peace with your own capacity for malevolence. Don't zealously assume the purity of your own motives.

RISE ABOVE YOUR MIND. The ability to think critically, reason, self-analyze, and self-criticize is far more important than being able to communicate, write, and speak. Introspect before you extrospect. Do not identify as your mind, but as the awareness eternally watching your mind. Do not be in your mind, but above it.

CLEAR THE FOG FROM YOUR PSYCHE. Know what you believe. Know your failures. Know your successes. Know your weaknesses. Know your strengths. Know what you fear. Know what you seek. Know your mind. Know yourself. Know your capacity for malevolence and evil. Know your capacity for goodness and greatness. Don't hide any part of yourself from yourself. Don't even try.

KNOW YOUR LOGOS. In 500 B.C. Heraclitus defined Logos as "that universal principle which animates and rules the world." What is your Logos? Meditate on it. Sit with it. Hold it up to the light, as a jeweler does with a gem, examining all angles.

KNOW YOUR LIMITS. The more you delineate and define the actions you consider unethical, the more likely you are to resist when they seem expedient.

REMEMBER THAT EVERYTHING MATTERS. There is no insignificant job, duty, role, mission, or speech. Everything matters. Everything seeks to beat back chaos in some way and create order. A laundromat doesn't deal in clean clothes, nor a trash disposal contractor in clean streets. They deal in order. In civilization. In human dignity. Don't ignore the reservoir of meaning and mattering upon which you stand. And remember that it is there, no matter where you stand.

GIVE THE GIFT OF MEANING. The greatest gift you can give to an audience is the gift of meaning; the knowledge that they matter, that they are irreplaceable.

HONOR YOUR INHERITANCE. You are the heir to thousands of years of human moralizing. Our world is shaped by the words of long-dead philosophers, and the gifts they gave us: gems of wisdom, which strengthen us against the dread and chaos of the world. We stand atop the pillars of 4,000 years of myth and meaning. Our arguments and moral compasses are not like planks of driftwood in a raging sea, but branches nourished by an inestimably old tree. Don't forget it.

BE THE PERSON YOU WANT TO BE SEEN AS. How do you want to be seen by your audience? How can you actually be that way, rather than just seeming to be?

HAVE TRUE ETHOS. Ethos is the audience's perception that the speaker has their best interests at heart. It's your job to make sure this perception is accurate.

CHANGE PLACES WITH YOUR AUDIENCE. Put yourself in their shoes, and then be the speaker you would want to listen to, the speaker worthy of your trust.

ACT AS THOUGH THE WHOLE WORLD IS WATCHING. Or as though a newspaper will publish a record of your actions. Or as though you're writing your autobiography with every action, every word, and even every thought. (You are).

ACT WITH AUDACIOUS HONOR. As did John McCain when he called Obama, his political opponent, "a decent family man, [and] citizen, that I just happen to have disagreements with." As did Socrates and Galileo when they refused to betray truth.

ADOPT A MECHANIC'S MENTALITY. Face your challenges the way a mechanic faces a broken engine; not drowning in emotion, but with objectivity and clarity. Identify the problem. Analyze the problem. Determine the solution. Execute the solution. If it works, celebrate. If not, repeat the cycle. This is true for both your inner and outer worlds: your fear of speaking, for example, is a specific problem with a specific fix, as are your destructive external rhetorical habits.

APPLY THE MASTERY PROCESS INTERNALLY. The four-step mastery process is not only for mastering your rhetoric, but also for striving toward internal mastery.

MARSHAL YOURSELF ALONG THE THREE AXES. To marshal means to place in proper rank or position – as in marshaling the troops – and to bring together and order in the most effective way. It is a sort of preparation. It begins with taking complete stock of what is available. Then, you order it. So, marshal yourself along three axes: the rhetorical axis (your points, arguments, rhetorical techniques, key phrases, etc.), the internal axis (your peace of mind, your internal principles, your mental climate, etc.), and the truth axis (your research, your facts, your logic, etc.).

PRACTICE ONE PUNCH 10,000 TIMES. As the martial arts adage says, "I fear not the man who practiced 10,000 punches once, but the man who practiced one punch 10,000 times." So it is with speaking skills and rhetorical techniques.

MULTIPLY YOUR PREPARATION BY TEN. Do you need to read a manuscript ten times to memorize it? Aim to read it 100 times. Do you need to research for one hour to grasp the subject of your speech? Aim to research for ten.

REMEMBER THE HIGHEST PRINCIPLE OF COMMUNICATION: the connection between speaker and audience – here, now – in this moment, in this place.

KNOW THERE'S NO SUCH THING AS A "SPEECH." All good communication is just conversation, with varying degrees of formality heaped on top. It's all just connection between consciousnesses. Every "difference" is merely superficial.

SEE YOURSELF IN OTHERS. What are you, truly? Rene Descartes came close to an answer in 1637, when he said "cogito, ego sum," I think therefore I am. The answer this seems to suggest is that your thoughts are most truly you. But your thoughts (and your character) change all the time. Something that never changes, arguably even during deep sleep, is awareness. Awareness is also the precondition for thought. A computer performs operations on information, but we don't say the computer "thinks." Why? Because it lacks awareness. So, I believe what makes you "you," most fundamentally, is your awareness, your consciousness. And if you accept this claim – which is by no means a mystical or religious one – then you must also see yourself in others. Because while the contents of everyone's consciousness is different, the consciousness itself is identical. How could it be otherwise?

FORGIVE. Yourself. Your mistakes. Your detractors. The past. The future. All.

FREE YOUR MIND. Many of the most challenging obstacles we face are thoughts living in our own minds. Identify these thoughts, and treat them like weeds in a garden. Restore the pristine poise of your mind, and return to equanimity.

LET. Let what has been be and what will be be. Most importantly, let what is be what is. Work to do what good you can do, and accept the outcome.

**FLOW.** Wikipedia defines a flow state as such: "a flow state, also known colloquially as being in the zone, is the mental state in which a person performing some activity is fully immersed in a feeling of energized focus, full involvement, and enjoyment in the process of the activity. In essence, flow is characterized by the complete absorption in what one does, and a resulting transformation in one's sense of time." Speaking in a flow state transports you and your audience outside of space and time. When I entered deep flow states during my speeches and debates, audience members would tell me that "it felt like time stopped." It felt that way for me too. Speaking in a flow state is a form of meditation. And it both leads to and results from these guidelines. Adhering to them leads to flow, and flow helps you adhere to them.

**MEDITATE.** Meditation brings your attention to the "here and now." It creates flow. Practice silence meditation, sitting in still silence and focusing on the motions of your mind, but knowing yourself as the entity watching the mind, not the mind itself. Practice aiming meditation, centering your noble aim in your mind, and focusing on the resulting feelings. (Also, speaking in flow is its own meditation).

**EMBARK ON THE GRAND ADVENTURE.** Take a place wherever you are. Develop influence and impact. Improve your status. Take on responsibility. Develop capacity and ability. Do scary things. Dare to leap into a high-stakes speech with no preparation if you must. Dare to trust your instincts. Dare to strive. Dare to lead. Dare to speak the truth freely, no matter how brutal it is. Be bold. Risk failure. Throw out your notes. The greatest human actions – those that capture our hearts and minds – occur on the border between chaos and order, where someone is daring to act and taking a chance when they know they could fall off the tightrope with no net below. Training wheels kill the sense of adventure. Use them if you need to, but only to lose them as soon as you can. Speak from the heart and trust yourself. Put yourself out there. Let people see the gears turning in your mind, let them see you grappling with your message in real time, taking an exploration in the moment. This is not an automaton doing a routine. It's not robotic or mechanical. That's too much order. It's also not unstructured nonsense. That's too much chaos. There is a risk of failure, mitigated not by training wheels, but by preparation. It is not a perfectly practiced routine, but someone pushing themselves just beyond their comfort zone, right at the cutting-edge of what they are capable of. It's not prescriptive. It's not safe either. The possibility that you could falter and fall in real-time calls out the best from you, and is gripping for the audience. It is also a thrilling adventure. Have faith in yourself, faith that you will say the right words when you need to. Don't think ahead, or backward. Simply experience the moment.

**BREAK THE SEVEN LAWS OF WEAKNESS.** If your goal is weakness, follow these rules. Seek to control what you can't control. Seek praise and admiration from others. Bend the truth to achieve your goals. Treat people as instruments in your game. Only commit to outer goals, not inner goals. Seek power for its own sake. Let anger and dissatisfaction fuel you in your pursuits, and pursue them frantically.

FAIL. Losses lead to lessons. Lessons lead to wins. If there's no chance of failure in your present task, you aren't challenging yourself. And if you aren't challenging yourself, you aren't growing. And that's the deepest and most enduring failure.

DON'T BETRAY YOURSELF. To know the truth and not say the truth is to betray the truth and to betray yourself. To know the truth, seek the truth, love the truth, and to speak the truth and speak it well, with poise and precision and power… this is to honor the truth, and to honor yourself. The choice is yours.

FOLLOW YOUR INNER LIGHT. As the Roman emperor and stoic philosopher Marcus Aurelius wrote in his private journal, "If thou findest in human life anything better than justice, truth, temperance, fortitude, and, in a word, anything better than thy own mind's self-satisfaction in the things which it enables thee to do according to right reason, and in the condition that is assigned to thee without thy own choice; if, I say, thou seest anything better than this, turn to it with all thy soul, and enjoy that which thou hast found to be the best. But if nothing appears to be better than [this], give place to nothing else." And as Kant said, treat humans as ends, not means.

JUDGE THEIR JUDGMENT. People *are* thinking of you. They *are* judging you. But what is their judgment to you? Nothing. (Compared to your self-judgment).

BREAK LESSER RULES IN THE NAME OF HIGHER RULES. Our values and moral priorities nest in a hierarchy, where they exist in relation to one another. Some are more important than others. If life compels a tradeoff between two moral principles, as it often does, this means there is a right choice. Let go the lesser of the two.

DON'T AVOID CONFLICT. Necessary conflict avoided is an impending conflict exacerbated. Slay the hydra when it has two heads, not twenty.

SEE THE WHOLE BOARD. Become wise in the ways of the world, and learned in the games of power and privilege people have been playing for tens of thousands of years. See the status-struggles and dominance-shuffling around you. See the chess board. But then opt to play a different game; a more noble game. The game of self-mastery. The game that transcends all other games. The worthiest game.

SERVE SOMETHING. Everyone has a master. Everyone serves something. Freedom is not the absence of service. Freedom is the ability to choose your service. What, to you, is worth serving? With your work and with your words?

TAKE RESPONSIBILITY FOR YOUR RIPPLE EFFECT. If you interact with 1,000 people, and they each interact with 1,000 more who also do the same, you are three degrees away from one billion people. Remember that compassion is contagious.

ONLY SPEAK WHEN YOUR WORDS ARE BETTER THAN SILENCE. And only write when your words are better than a blank page.

KNOW THERE IS THAT WHICH YOU DON'T KNOW YOU DON'T KNOW. Of course, there's that you know you don't know too. Recognize the existence of both of these domains of knowledge, which are inaccessible to you in your present state.

REMEMBER THAT AS WITHIN, SO (IT APPEARS) WITHOUT. If you orient your aim toward goals fueled by emotions like insecurity, jealousy, or vengeance, the world manifests itself as a difficult warzone. If you orient your aim toward goals fueled by emotions like universal compassion and positive ambition, the beneficence of the world manifests itself to you. Your aim and your values alter your perception.

ORIENT YOUR AIM PROPERLY. Actions flow from thought. Actions flow from *motives*. If you orient your aim properly – if you aim at the greatest good for the greatest number, at acting forthrightly and honorably – then this motive will fuel right actions, subconsciously, automatically, and without any forethought.

STOP TRYING TO USE SPEECH TO GET WHAT YOU WANT. Try to articulate what you believe to be true as carefully as possible, and then accept the outcome.

LEARN THE MEANING OF WHAT YOU SAY. Don't assume you already know.

USE THE MOST POWERFUL "RHETORICAL" TACTIC. There is no rhetorical tool more powerful than the overwhelming moral force of the unvarnished truth.

INJECT YOUR EXPERIENCE INTO YOUR SPEECH. Speak of what you know and testify of what you have seen. Attach your philosophizing and persuading and arguing to something real, some story you lived through, something you've seen.

DETACH FROM OUTCOME. As Stoic philosopher Epictetus said: "There is only one way to happiness and that is to cease worrying about things which are beyond the power of our will. Make the best use of what is in your power, and take the rest as it happens. The essence of philosophy is that a man should so live that his happiness shall depend as little as possible on external things. Remember to conduct yourself in life as if at a banquet. As something being passed around comes to you, reach out your hand and take a moderate helping. Does it pass you? Don't stop it. It hasn't yet come? Don't burn in desire for it, but wait until it arrives in front of you."

FOCUS ON WHAT YOU CONTROL. As Epictetus said, "It's not what happens to you, but how you react to it that matters. You may be always victorious if you will never enter into any contest where the issue does not wholly depend upon yourself. Some things are in our control and others not. Things in our control are opinion, pursuit, desire, aversion, and, in a word, whatever are our own actions. Things not in our control are body, property, reputation, command, and, in one word, whatever are not our own actions. Men are disturbed not by things, but by the view which they take of them. God has entrusted me with myself. Do not with that all things will go well with you, but that you will go well with all things." Before a high-stakes speech or event, I always tell myself this: "All I want from this, all I aim at, is to conduct what I control, my thoughts and actions, to the best of my ability. Any external benefit I earn is merely a bonus."

VIEW YOURSELF AS A VESSEL. Conduct yourself as something through which truth, brilliantly articulated, flows into the world; not as a self-serving entity, but a conduit for something higher. Speak not for your glory, but for the glory of good.

Want to Talk? Email Me:

**PANDREIBUSINESS@GMAIL.COM**

This is My Personal Email.
I Read Every Message and
Respond in Under 12 Hours.

Made in the USA
Las Vegas, NV
15 December 2023

82843766R00134